The Great Auditorium

OCEAN GROVE'S ARCHITECTURAL TREASURE

Articles of Agreement and Specifications
of the Auditorium in Ocean Grove, NJ

WAYNE T. BELL, JR.

CINDY L. BELL

DARRELL A. DUFRESNE

the Peppertree Press
Sarasota, Florida

For information regarding permission,
call 941-922-2662 or contact us at our website:
www.peppertreepublishing.com or write to:
the Peppertree Press, LLC.
Attention: Publisher
1269 First Street, Suite 7
Sarasota, Florida 34236

ISBN: 978-1-61493-036-5

Library of Congress Number: 2012933695

Printed in the U.S.A.

Printed May 2012

The glory of this latter house
shall be greater than the former,
saith the Lord of hosts.

Haggai 2:9

as quoted by Rev. Dr. Ellwood H. Stokes on Sunday, July 1, 1894.

Examples of ticket stubs from various shows in the Auditorium.

Table of Contents

Background and List of Contracts

Wayne T. Bell, Jr.

In 1999, I decided to develop a brochure on Fredrick Theodore Camp, the architect of the 10,000 seat, wood-and-steel frame Auditorium built in 1893-1894 on the camp meeting grounds of Ocean Grove in Monmouth County, NJ. The brochure was to be four-fold, illustrated with Camp's picture, a history of his life and a few notes on the Auditorium. What originally began as a small research project on the architect of the Auditorium evolved into a full accounting of the Auditorium's history, construction and changes that have occurred to the building over the last 118 years. Now, having traveled a few thousand miles and accumulated about three cubic feet of written material, notes, pictures, books and e-mails on the Auditorium itself, I have an extensive study of the building, but little material on the architect. Despite several potential leads, I am unable to locate Fred Camp's descendants or find the elusive photo of the architect of the Auditorium.

The *Articles of Agreements and Specifications* are the result of an accidental encounter with Monmouth County Archivist Gary Saretzky while visiting the Monmouth County Archives in Manalapan, NJ. Gary, in his quiet and unassuming way, asked what project I was working on and I told him that I was researching an architect, Fred Camp, who designed the Auditorium in Ocean Grove. "We might have something on him," Gary said, and twenty minutes later his staff laid on the veneer rosewood conference table a legal size acid-free folder with the name "Frederick T. Camp" on the tab.

The folder contained 86 pages of original agreements and specifications on the construction of the Auditorium, signed in 1893-1894, and sealed by Reverend Ellwood H. Stokes, President of the Ocean Grove Camp Meeting Association, and Frederick T. Camp, Architect. As far as we know, this is the only copy of the Auditorium specifications and construction. What a treasure!! My original project was temporarily shelved, as I turned my attention to the building and design of the Auditorium.

Some items on construction are missing, but the gaps are filled by information available in newspaper articles, minutes of meetings and reports. There is always the chance that new material will be found that corrects or adds to this present book. Occasionally, there were conflicting numbers and dates, for example, the number of seats in the Auditorium. The seat numbers are discussed in Chapter 7. Where possible, we chose the most logical.

For those interested in the construction of the Auditorium, this material is presented here with old and new pictures, etchings and summaries of the individual contracts and specifications. It was decided to copy all the contracts in the original 8.5 by 14 inch legal size and then reduce to 8.5 by 11 inches, for ease of reading. In many instances we incorporated the original contract wording in the chapter summaries. Also included are portions of the 1892, 1893 and 1894 Annual Reports of the OGCMA, written by Stokes, as an additional guide and reference.

Unfortunately, contracts for certain works are missing and may not have been filed at the Monmouth County Clerk's office, but their names are listed in the 1894 Annual Report of the OGCMA as follows:

Lumber Supplies:	Charles Lewis and Buchanon & Smock, Ocean Grove, NJ
Master Mason:	Titian P. Summers, Ocean Grove, NJ
Corrugated Iron Roof:	C. W. Carll, Trenton, NJ
Architect:	Frederick Theodore Camp, New York, NY

Also missing is the 1893-1894 Day Book on Construction Changes, kept by the Clerk of the Works, Wistar H. Stokes.

The following is a subject list of the contract amounts, date signed and projected date of completion that were awarded to the various successful bidders:

AUDITORIUM CONTRACTS

SUBJECT	CONTRACT AMOUNT	DATE SIGNED	DATE TO BE COMPLETED
Architect Frederick T. Camp	Unknown	Oct. 10, 1893 Awarded Commission	
Iron-Work	$15,500	Nov. 29, 1893	March 15, 1894
		Dec. 8, 1893	Bond of Samuel Milliken
		Jan. 5, 1894	Steel Specifications
Plumbing	$175.00	Dec. 12, 1893	May 15, 1894
Painting	$1,545	Dec. 15, 1893	May 15, 1894
Seats	$3,600	Dec. 30, 1893	June 20, 1894
Carpentry/Metal Roof	$26,000	Jan. 13, 1894	June 20, 1894
Electric	$1,248	May 5, 1894	June 16, 1894
Total Contracts	$48,068		

The forms used for these contracts were standard preprinted forms by Palliser, Palliser and Company, New York, publisher of house and architectural plan books of the 1890's. We invite you to read and enjoy all the *Articles of Agreement and Specifications* contracts immediately following each subject chapter. These are a testament to the design and thought that went into the construction of the Auditorium by architect Frederick T. Camp.

The simplicity and beauty of this Camp Meeting building speaks for itself.

Foreword

COMMENTS ON RODS, CABLES, DOMES, ARCHES, BUTTRESSES AND WHY THE
ROMANS COULD NOT BUILD THE OCEAN GROVE AUDITORIUM

Darrell A. Dufresne

Man has been putting together buildings from his early beginnings. Early on, it was relatively easy to build a small hut for a family to escape from bad weather. A few pliant small trees with the ends of their trunks stuck in the ground in a circle, bent over and tied together in the center could be covered with branches, bark, mud, hides, etc., and a cozy, strong house appeared. It was apparently intuitive that a hut in the shape of a dome would be strong and simple to construct. But, as societies evolved, it seemed like a good idea to have bigger buildings for communal use. The obvious expedient of building a really big hut didn't work. Trees, used to build the skeleton, were too short or too stiff to bend into a dome or arch shape. A really big dome also had the inconvenient habit of falling down. One successful approach to the falling down problem was to add vertical poles inside the hut to hold the roof up. This did solve the falling down problem but the poles got in the way.

Time marched on, civilization continued its evolution, and cities grew. The Greeks, and later the Romans, wanted big buildings. Their one approach was to use an arch which would carry the load to the ground in much the same way the hut worked. They even discovered that many arches could be placed next to each other and the barrel vault was invented. This resulted in long buildings with no central poles but they had to be built low and quite narrow. Another issue with huts and barrel vaults was that openings, like windows, had to be kept to a minimum as they weakened the structure - and the building would fall down. As a result, large buildings were long, narrow and dark. Without the ventilation that larger windows would provide, these buildings had other unpleasant issues.

The Romans also built square or rectangular buildings as we can still see in places like Pompeii and Herculaneum which were preserved by the eruption of Vesuvius in the year 79 A.D. These buildings, houses and baths, were large but the internal space was cut-up by walls that marked rooms or by columns that held up the roof. Where a large room was needed, like in a bath house, a barrel vault was used. Man had big buildings but not buildings with vast open interiors. A popular big building design was the basilica, which in Roman times meant a long, rectangular public building. Forums had basilicas to house government activities. These were generally full of columns to support the ceiling.

The Romans also knew that the shape of the original hut, the dome, was inherently strong and they cut stones and concrete to build them. The second century A.D. emperor Hadrian dabbled in architecture and designed a remarkable domed building in Rome, the Pantheon. The Pantheon is a large round, 142 foot diameter building with a dome on top. The problem encountered by the Romans with domes up high is that outward forces push the ends of the dome and the walls out and the building falls down. Hadrian dealt with this by building very thick walls and an amazingly light dome, with a 27 foot diameter hole in its center. The dome was lightened by making it thinner as it rose to its top, by molding in square recesses and by mixing light weight

The interior of the Pantheon in Rome is free from supports. The diameter of the dome and the height to the oculus are each 142 feet.

The dome and the oculus of the Pantheon in Rome. Note the square recesses which lighten the weight of the dome.

volcanic material into the concrete. Still an amazing building, the Pantheon has no internal supports and its wide open interior awed the Roman citizenry and still amazes its visitors today. But the Pantheon pretty well represented the limit; it was not practicable to go bigger.

It was centuries following the fall of Rome, and the loss of its architectural knowledge, before man again tried to build really big buildings. The impact of the loss of the Roman's architectural knowledge is better understood by the realization that concrete was not re-discovered until 1756 A.D., about 13 centuries later. Christianity and its desire for great cathedrals to the glory of God led the next significant venture into big buildings. The lessons of the past were re-learned as larger and larger cathedrals were attempted. The arch, the dome (hut), and the vault all wound up in the cathedrals. What was not available to the builders of the great cathedrals was concrete. As cathedrals were raised to greater heights and bigger interiors, they had a tendency to fail. They had the general shape of the Roman basilica - actually two of these form a transept.

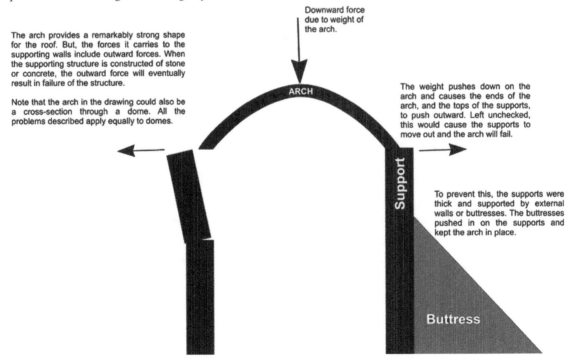

The arch provides a remarkably strong shape for the roof. But, the forces it carries to the supporting walls include outward forces. When the supporting structure is constructed of stone or concrete, the outward force will eventually result in failure of the structure.

Note that the arch in the drawing could also be a cross-section through a dome. All the problems described apply equally to domes.

Downward force due to weight of the arch.

ARCH

The weight pushes down on the arch and causes the ends of the arch, and the tops of the supports, to push outward. Left unchecked, this would cause the supports to move out and the arch will fail.

Support

To prevent this, the supports were thick and supported by external walls or buttresses. The buttresses pushed in on the supports and kept the arch in place.

Buttress

At the Notre Dame Cathedral, the very thin exterior wall supports are actually one-half of an arch. The great amount of wall pierced for windows was possible because the tops of the window frames are arches.

Roofs presented forces that pushed the walls apart and, weakened by their height, they tended to fail and the buildings threatened to fall down. To prevent this, many internal support columns and buttresses were added. Buttresses were walls built perpendicular to the cathedral walls to hold them in place and prevent them from falling. Roof supports and walls were made from stone, big stones, and were heavy. It was not a good idea to cut large holes in the walls for windows because this would weaken the walls and, you guessed it, the building would fall down. Also, the buttresses were big and thick and blocked the sun light even if there were big windows.

The arch came to the rescue. Windows could be bigger if they were arch shaped, roof support structures could be stronger and lighter if they were made up of arch shapes and the buttresses could let in a lot more light if, instead of being solid, they were ½ arches. The ½ arch buttress is called a flying buttress. Notre Dame Cathedral, an amazing example, was completed in about 1345 A.D. – still four centuries before concrete was available.

So, the great cathedrals were realized by application of arches, domes and vaults, lighter building materials and really thick, massive walls. Advances were very slow after that, due to the lack of building materials with a critical capability. The missing ability was tensile strength - that is, the strength to resist being pulled apart. Stone, brick and even concrete all are very strong in compression, that is, when a force is trying to crush them. If these materials are presented with forces trying to pull them apart, however, they fail relatively easily. What was needed was steel or, early on, iron. The dome of Saint Peter's Basilica in Vatican City and its supporting walls had begun to be pushed outward and would have failed if not rescued. In the mid-18th century, cracks appeared in the dome, so four iron chains were installed between the two shells to bind it, like the rings that keep a barrel from bursting. As many as ten chains have been installed at various times.

Two examples of the crossed rods at the top tier of windows. The left photograph, showing author Ted Bell, is inside on the south wall. The right photograph was taken of the outside rear on the west. The crossed rods, present in every other window, actually connect between two of the vertical steel supports. They are solidly anchored and tightened. The vertical columns remain parallel and thus prevent the building from falling even in high winds.

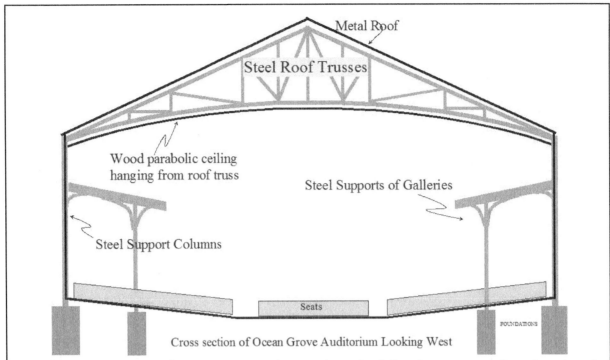

Metal Roof

Steel Roof Trusses

Wood parabolic ceiling hanging from roof truss

Steel Supports of Galleries

Steel Support Columns

Seats

FOUNDATIONS

Cross section of Ocean Grove Auditorium Looking West

Cross-section of Auditorium. There are no supports between the roof and floor, just open space for a clear view of Auditorium performances. The ceiling is simply hung from the arches. The roof trusses with their integral arches carry all of the roof weight to the vertical supports in the side walls. Hidden in plain sight is the gallery or balcony, buttresses which are inside the building and do double duty by supporting the floor of the balconies. These keep the walls (actually the vertical support columns) from moving in or out.

A look at the Ocean Grove Auditorium appears to defy the need for arches. It is a rectangular building with no sign of structural arches, buttresses, domes, vaults or any of the aforementioned architectural necessities. But, the arches and vaults are there. The function of the buttresses is provided, but it is hidden inside the building. Most, but not all, of these are hidden from view. Take a look inside the Auditorium; there are no internal roof supports, the ceiling just appears to float up there. The answer is in the steel.

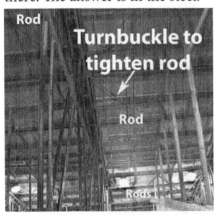

Rod

Turnbuckle to tighten rod

Rod

Rods

This view of the space above the Auditorium ceiling shows some of the arch and truss structure. To prevent these from moving in wind stresses, steel rods are connected between adjacent trusses and tightened with turnbuckles. The Auditorium doesn't move around, even in high winds.

The Ocean Grove Auditorium is not built of wood, even though it appears to be. It is not a cubic rectangle with a pitched roof, even though it looks like that. The Auditorium is a steel building that gets its basic strength from arches and cables or rods. The wood is just hung on the steel skeleton. Because of this the Auditorium has many very large openings to admit fresh cool air.

Visible inside the Auditorium, or outside, when the top row of windows is open, at every second top window is an "X" across. This is part of the secret of the building's strength and evidence of the use of the building material the Romans and their successors didn't have: steel. Steel is a critical ingredient in modern architecture. It provides great strength-to-weight ratio and it is strong in tension. A strong, light weight material that resists

A turnbuckle, stretching screw or **bottle-screw** *is a device for adjusting the tension or length of rods and other tensioning systems. It normally consists of two threaded rods, one screwed into each end of a small metal frame, one with a left-hand thread and the other with a right-hand thread. The length can be adjusted by rotating the frame, which causes both eyelets to be screwed in or out simultaneously.*

being pulled apart, the Romans could not conceive of it and we would not have the Ocean Grove Auditorium without it.

Here is how it works. The Auditorium is considerably taller than it looks to be from the inside. Actually, due to the shape of the roof, it is actually taller than it appears on the outside, too. The secret of the Auditorium's construction is for the most part hidden in the immense space above the ceiling. In that space are hidden the arches, some vault-like structures, and cables or rods that eliminate the need for buttresses. All this is implemented in steel. To understand how the Auditorium works, visualize the building in cross section looking from the east, as if you were standing on Ocean Pathway, with the front half of the building removed. What you see is steel arches above the ceiling. These steel arches are the bottom of great trusses and provide support to the roof and the ceiling. The truss structure with the arched bottom profile provides a rigid, strong structure. Using steel and the advantage of modern engineering these structures provide what the Romans and later builders could not accomplish - an arch that does not push outward on its supporting walls. The Auditorium's arches don't even rest on the building's walls at all. Each of the arches is supported on its ends by steel vertical "I" Shaped columns, which in turn rest on concrete bases. (The contribution of the re-invention of concrete should not be forgotten.) There are a total of 7 arches resting on 32 foot high steel columns.

Without some added support, a 32 foot long vertical pole will tend to flex as a result of forces at its top from, for example, wind. To control movement in the direction across the building, each truss structure provides a rigid member. To prevent the arches from moving with respect to each other, steel members, including rods in tension, connect one to the other at top and bottom. With the elements connected together, independent motion of components is prevented. To stiffen the entire structure, the rods that cross at the top windows, as noted earlier, are added. These rods connect the top of each steel column in a pair to the side of the other one. These rods are tightened and keep the columns parallel resulting in a rigid member. These crossed rods are re-peated between every second pair of columns on the sides and rear of the Auditorium.

We still have the buttresses, but they are hard to find. They are hidden in plain sight. The Auditorium has a balcony (gallery) on the north and south sides and the rear wall. In the sketch of the Auditorium cross section, the galleries look like buttresses except that they are on the *inside* of the building. These help to hold the walls up by pulling in on them. Unlike external buttresses, they are in tension.

So now you know why the Romans, and their successors, could not build the Ocean Grove Auditorium and why we could: steel, concrete, and tension from rods and cables.

This picture shows the crossed rods in the top tier of the south side of the Auditorium. The black X shows the hidden portion of the rods, and where they are tied to the steel columns.

The Osborn Cottage is a typical two-story wood-framed cottage surrounded by a white picket fence. On July 15, 1873, this cottage, costing over $3,000, was a gift to Rev. Osborn from his friends in acknowledgment of his leadership and labors rendered in the founding of Ocean Grove

Chapter One

In The Beginning: Ocean Grove

William Osborn, Founder

The Rev. William B. Osborn (1832-1902), who is considered the founder of Ocean Grove, is well known for his role in the National Holiness Association, formed in 1867 at a camp meeting in Vineland, NJ. So successful was the Vineland revival that Osborn looked to expand the National Holiness Association with additional camp meetings sites. For two years, he searched along the New Jersey coast, but rejected grounds at Seven Mile Beach, Cape May County, because of the high mosquito population. In 1868, Osborn made a winter visit to a parcel of land in Monmouth County on the sparsely populated North Jersey Shore, about ten miles south of Long Branch. The site – bordered on two sides by lakes and on the east by the Atlantic Ocean - seemed ideal to establish a permanent camp meeting: "the highest beach, best grove, and the place free from mosquitoes."

On July 30, 1869, Osborn led a group of ministers and lay people to camp in tents at Long Pond (Wesley Lake), in what is now known as Founders Park. The next evening at an informal prayer meeting, in the tent of Mrs. Joseph H. Thornley, the group dedicated themselves to creating a permanent camp meeting site called "Ocean Grove."

In December 1869, this group – now formally called the Ocean Grove Camp Meeting Association of the Methodist Episcopal Church - held its first organizational meeting in Trenton, New Jersey, and elected Rev. Ellwood H. Stokes as its first president. On March 3, 1870, the State of New Jersey Legislature issued a Charter to the OGCMA "for the purpose of providing and maintaining, for the members and friends of the Methodist Episcopal Church, a proper, convenient and desirable permanent camp meeting ground and Christian seaside resort."

The Charter granted the 26 Trustees (13 ministers and 13 lay people) the "authority to purchase and hold real and personal estate, to construct and provide all necessary works to supply said

Rev. William B. Osborn (1832-1902), founder of Ocean Grove. In 1857 he dedicated his life's work to Christian evangelism in a camp meeting setting. A strong-willed person with auburn red hair, he felt it was his "great work to originate (camp meetings) but it was not his function to develop them."

premises with water and artificial light and other improvements as deemed necessary or desirable." The Charter also gave the trustees the power to appoint peace officers as deemed necessary for the purpose of keeping order on the camp grounds and premises of the corporation.

Osborn was the first superintendent of the grounds, but his developmental enthusiasm knew no bounds, and he was soon involved in other ventures. When Osborn left Ocean Grove in 1872 to do missionary work elsewhere, the Camp Meeting had increased in size from the original six acres to 230 acres. Beyond Ocean Grove he founded 11 other permanent camp meeting grounds (annual events) and 30 other camp meeting assemblies. He even founded a camp meeting named "Ocean Grove" in Australia and one at Lanowli in India. His remarkable history is available elsewhere.

Ellwood Haines Stokes, First President

Ellwood Haines Stokes, D.D., was born on October 10, 1815, of Quaker parents in Medford, Burlington County, New Jersey. The family moved to Philadelphia in 1826, and at age thirteen, Stokes became an indentured apprentice to a bookbinder at a salary of one dollar a week. His love of books would continue with him throughout his life. He was an avid journal writer, including an autobiography *"Footprints in My Own Life,"* several accounts of his travels and books of poetry. His conversion to Methodism occurred in 1834 after a moving sermon by Charles Pitman, an early revival preacher.

The statue of Rev. Ellwood Haines Stokes by sculptor Paul W. Morris faces the Atlantic Ocean.

Stokes entered the New Jersey Conference in April 1844 and served as pastor in Newark, Morristown, New Brunswick, Trenton, Bordentown and Camden. He was one of the presiding elders in the New Jersey Conference from 1867 to 1875. Stokes was chosen president of the Ocean Grove Camp Meeting Association (OGCMA) at its organizational meeting in Trenton on December 22, 1869. He continued in this leadership position until his death in Ocean Grove at age 82 on July 17, 1897.

Stokes' life was one of holiness with great practicality and foresight. In his role as OGCMA President, he was the main author for 26 years of the Ocean Grove Annual Reports. His greatest achievements were his leadership of Ocean Grove in its beginning years and the construction of the 1894 Auditorium, and his finest memorial is the permanent Camp Meeting of Ocean Grove.

A heroic-size bronze statue of Rev. Stokes is located on Ocean Pathway facing east toward the Atlantic Ocean. Stokes is sitting in a chair with his left arm resting on an open Bible on a side stand. At the base of the pedestal stand are four symbols: an ox, a lion, a winged messenger and an eagle. Cast in 1905 by sculptor Paul W. Morris, the cost for the $6,000 statue was raised through donations by his many friends.

Camp Meetings

Almost all early camp meeting activities centered in or around a brush arbor, a large canvas tent or an open-air, barn-like wooden structure. Here, religious services were held three or four times a day for a seven to ten day period in the warm months of the summer. Some camp meetings were officially sponsored by Methodist Churches, others were not. Baptist and Presbyterians also had similar arrangements although not as intense as the Methodist. In 1854, the Reverend B. W. Gorham published a manual of detailed plans and descriptions of camp meetings and suggested camp meeting activities. Camp meetings were considered as temporary church encampments for a summer gathering in a forest setting. A gentle slope or ravine was a preferred site as it did not involve major site alterations and it provided worshipers with good viewing of the preacher's stand. All camp meetings had a preacher's stand, a "mourners" or "anxiety bench" and an altar where sinners could kneel and pray for forgiveness. The shape of the camp meeting grounds was carefully planned and the most common shapes included an open horseshoe, a circle or a rectangle, but again the site's topography determined the final configuration.

The original 1870 Ocean Grove plan called for two locations for assemblies, both in rectangular shapes. The first area, labeled

A large canvas tent – true camp meeting style - is shown in this early photo of Ocean Grove.

With no cover except for the shade of oak and pitch pine trees, the rustic appearance of the camp meeting only enhanced the revival activities. The area was kept clean by the ladies dresses sweeping the grounds bare.

"Tabernacle," is located on the north end of the camp meeting, where Long Pond (Wesley Lake) meets the Atlantic Ocean. The other site, in the middle of the tenting grounds, is labeled "Church Square." Apparently, this early north end Tabernacle site was abandoned as it no longer is present on the 1871 map. Perhaps this assembly site was moved to the Pavilion, located at Ocean Pathway and Ocean Avenue, because it is from this location that the earliest etchings and stereopticon photographs of evening beach sermon meetings are recorded.

The following daily schedule for camp meeting activities by Reverend B. W. Gorham (1854) is typical of camp meetings:

The initial plan shows the layout of 30 by 60 foot lots from Lake Avenue to Main Avenue. Sea Drift Heights and Ladies Walk are two coastal dunes that functioned as comfort areas. They were eventually leveled and utilized elsewhere for fill.

Worship and Atonement:

1. Rise at five, or half past five in the morning.
2. Family prayer and breakfast from half-past six to half-past seven.
3. General prayer meeting at the altar, led by several ministers appointed by the Presiding Elder, at half-past eight, a.m.
4. Preaching at half-past ten, followed by prayer meeting to twelve, p.m.
5. Dine at half-past twelve, p.m.
6. Preaching at two, or half-past two, p.m., followed by prayer at the altar till five.
7. Tea at six, p.m.
8. Preaching at half-past seven, followed by prayer meeting at the altar till nine or ten.
9. All strangers to leave the ground and the people to retire at ten, or immediately thereafter.

In Ocean Grove, the ringing of a sweet tone bell announced preaching times. Rules were strictly enforced due to the large number of attendees at the camp meetings.

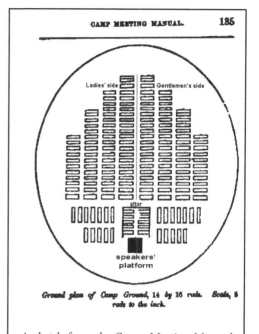

A sketch from the Camp Meeting Manual by Rev. B. W. Gorham (1854). Tents and wagons were located outside of the revival circle. Men and women were seated in separate sections for the services.

Definitions

It is helpful to examine the building terminology utilized by Ocean Grove's early leaders, since half of them were ordained ministers. The word "tabernacle" has its origin in ancient writings and in Jewish history and means "tent dwelling" or "tent of the congregation." A detailed description of a Jewish tabernacle can be found in the Bible in Exodus, Chapters 25-27.

A "pavilion" is a building or part of a building generally partially open and used for exhibits, entertainment and lectures. In Ocean Grove, the "Church Square" became the Auditorium with a preacher's stand at its center, surrounded by the congregation sitting on pine plank settees. An "auditorium" is defined as a building or hall for speeches, concerts, religious services, etc. Tabernacle, pavilion and auditorium are not interchangeable terms even though all three structures can cover a large space, whether constructed of canvas, tree branches, wood beams, brick, steel, glass or a combination thereof. Today, these three terms are used to identify specific buildings in Ocean Grove.

The Auditorium in Ocean Grove is not officially a Methodist church. The word "church" is from the Greek "kyrios," meaning Lord's (House) or a body of Christian people. The Camp Meeting Association is a private, non-profit self-supporting religious organization, with strong ties to Protestant denominations, particularly the United Methodist Church. However, in the true sense of the word "church," the people who attend and support the Ocean Grove Camp Meeting Association are, indeed, a "body of Christian people."

Engraving of a Sabbath evening service at the seaside pavilion on Ocean Pathway. The preacher had to be in strong voice to be heard over the sound of crashing waves.

The Auditorium in Ocean Grove

The center of the Ocean Grove Camp Meeting Association is the Auditorium. This massive wooden building, with a combination of late Queen Anne, Victorian and Gothic styles, is truly unique in camp meeting history. The Auditorium is located 1,500 feet west of the Atlantic Ocean at the head of Ocean Pathway. This vista from the ocean to the Auditorium enforces and effectively states the religious nature of the camp meeting. In the summer one has to walk the hot, open, three block promenade to reach the shaded cool woods surrounding the Auditorium. This walk on the pathway could be considered as reinforcement that the path to redemption and salvation requires some unpleasantness and sacrifice. The environmental benefits of this location, enhanced by the exchange of sea and land breezes, will be discussed in Chapter 9 on Ventilation.

In his original site plan for the town, Osborn created the "set back," a flaring effect (design) for the first two blocks from the ocean. Each building in the first two blocks is "set back" a specific distance from the street, so that each porch has a clear view of the ocean. For example, the width of Ocean Pathway at Ocean Avenue is 300 feet while the width of Ocean Pathway at Central Avenue is 200 feet, thus creating a "set back" or "flaring effect."

Vistas are intended to make statements of power and beauty. Other examples of vistas include the Washington, D.C., mall and the gardens from the terrace at Versailles in France. This aerial photo postcard (1965) illustrates the design and importance of the Ocean Grove Pathway vista.

There is a debate as to who actually designed the set back concept for the first two blocks from Ocean Avenue to Central Avenue. Was it Frederick H. Kennedy and Son, a civil engineering and surveying firm in Deal, New Jersey, or was it Rev. William Osborn, the first superintendent and founder of Ocean Grove? The early Annual Reports acknowledge the efforts of both men in the initial preparation of the site to have the first lease/sale of 100 lots by June 1, 1870, just three months after acquiring the charter. One answer to this question is suggested by Mrs. Lucy Reed Drake

HEADQUARTERS OF THE NEW YORK STATE CENTENNIAL BOARD AT FAIRMOUNT PARK, PHILADELPHIA.

The New York Centennial Building designed by Croft and Camp at the 1876 Centennial Exposition in Philadelphia. The two story wooden structure with cupola and wide veranda is typical of mid-Victorian design.

Osborn in her book *Pioneer Days of Ocean Grove* where she states "It was with great difficulty that Mr. Osborn (her husband) secured the consent of the Association to devote so much land to Ocean Pathway (now its crowning glory)."

Frederick Theodore Camp, Auditorium Architect

Frederick Theodore Camp was born on July 16, 1849, in Burlington, Vermont, a grandson of Bishop John Henry Hopkins, who was one of the early Episcopal Bishops in America. Bishop Hopkins' interests and leadership included the development of academic schools under church sponsorship, abolition of slavery, design and construction of church buildings, music and painting. Bishop Hopkins' son, John Henry Hopkins, Jr., is the composer of the Christmas carol *We Three Kings*.

Based on what is available, it appears that Frederick Camp's early education was at the Vermont Episcopal Institute, home schooling and apprenticeships. His father, Rev. Norman Camp, served at various Episcopal churches in Hoboken, Hudson and Trenton in New Jersey and New York City, and as a civil war chaplain in Washington, DC, in 1863. In 1876, the architectural firm of Gilbert Croft and Frederick Camp designed the New York State building at the 1876 Centennial Exposition in Philadelphia. Later, Croft and Camp designed several brick stores and homes for various clients in St. John, New Brunswick, Canada, where a disastrous fire had destroyed most of the town. Camp also designed in St. John a stone church for an Episcopal congregation at a cost that did not exceed $10,000.

The partnership apparently ended in 1880 when Camp opened a separate New York office and began working with various clients on Park Avenue and Columbus Avenue in New York City. His designs were mostly five to eight story apartment buildings, stores and private homes. In 1882 he published a 44-page book entitled "Draftsman's Manual or How Can I Learn Architecture? Hints to Enquirers, Directions in Draftsmanship." In 1883, he designed the "Imperial" at 55 East 76 Street in New York. This innovative, seven-story brownstone French Flat (Neo-Greco in appearance) was complete with an elevator and a fire fighting system for each floor. In 1888, he designed the Bishop Hopkins Hall in Rock Point, Vermont, a Richardson-style sandstone school building in memory of his grandfather. Other works included five, six and seven-story brick flats along Amsterdam Avenue in New York City, and other New Jersey projects such as his Victorian home at 187 Broad Street in Bloomfield, New Jersey. Unfortunately, his architectural design career was cut short, as he died at age 56 at home on September 19, 1905.

In fall 1893, Camp won the competition for the design of the 9,600-seat camp meeting Auditorium at Ocean Grove. His design was one of 15 that were submitted to the OGCMA as the result of a solicitation of bids notice in the regional newspapers. The 1894 Auditorium stands today as one of Camp's lasting architectural achievements.

DRAFTSMAN'S MANUAL;

OR,

"HOW CAN I LEARN ARCHITECTURE?"

HINTS TO ENQUIRERS.

DIRECTIONS IN DRAFTSMANSHIP.

NEW REVISED AND ENLARGED EDITION.

BY

F. T. CAMP,

ARCHITECT.

WILLIAM T. COMSTOCK,
194 BROADWAY, NEW YORK.

1882.

The cover page of the 1882 Draftsman's Manual written by Auditorium architect Fred T. Camp.

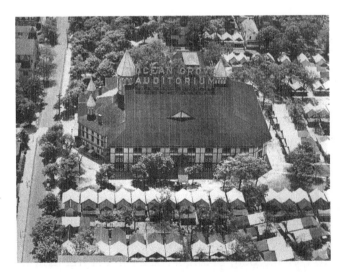

Aerial view of the Auditorium surrounded by the colony of 114 tents. The large metal sign "OCEAN GROVE AUDITORIUM" was removed in 1979.

The 1894 Auditorium

When viewed west from the boardwalk in 1894, the Auditorium appeared as a church-like structure of Gothic style. The impressive, rectangular three-story wooden building occupies an area 225 feet in length by 161 feet in width or 36,225 square feet. The outline of the building is defined by four towers, three at the east front and one at the west rear. The central octagonal tower – 18 feet in diameter with pointed arch louver vents – is recessed from the front of the building and has a height of 119 feet as it soars above the 84 feet high center roof line. Two smaller octagonal east towers, 62 feet in height and 8 feet in diameter, are positioned in front and to the sides of the main tower. The rear, or west, tower is 102 feet in height and 14 feet in diameter and is square in shape. All towers have lanced-shaped louvers on each side, for ventilation purposes.

As pedestrians approached the Auditorium from Ocean Pathway, they were welcomed by two porch entrances on the ground level. A third, smaller porch on the south side broke the symmetry of the front façade. Above the porch roof were eight 10-foot high Gothic style windows with colored glass panes, set off by a band of 20 zinc metal ornamental wreaths, evenly spaced along the front cornice. On both sides of the smaller towers were a double set of similar style colored windows. Early postcards show two yellow brick chimneys adjacent to these towers.

Over the years, particularly in 1907-1908, with the installation of the Hope-Jones organ, alterations were made to the front of the Auditorium

The 1894 dedication photo of the Auditorium. Note the Queen Anne style chimneys positioned next to the smaller twin towers. One of the Fisk cast iron urns is now located at the corner of Broadway and Central Avenue.

with a one story addition built on top of the existing porches. It featured a new roof which was aligned with the existing roof at the mid point of the bell towers. As a result of this addition, the lower half of the two smaller towers and all of the arched colored glass windows were covered. A janitor's residence and an office were also added.

On both the north and south sides of the Auditorium are three tiers of movable barn-like door panels, 32 feet in total height. The panels on the first tier or ground floor are readily movable so that the entire first tier is completely open for access to summer breezes. The second and third tiers can be opened or closed as the weather dictates. On the west side only the first and third tier doors are present.

Queen Anne style construction is evident in the exterior woodwork of the Auditorium. Permanent side panels, which constitute about 40% of the building, are in patterns of mixed horizontal and vertical arrangements; horizontal on the second tier and vertical on the third tier. The three tiers of movable doors feature ornamental stick work and colored-glass windows of varying numbers of glass panes (4 panes by 4 panes first tier, and 4 panes by 2 panes second tier). The third tier sliding doors have a total of 22 panes of colored glass per set of doors.

Inside the building, the wooden ceiling is parabolic in nature. The center height of the main ceiling reaches 55 feet from the ground floor. The height from the ceiling to the peak of the roof is 29 feet for a total of 84 feet. Wainscot strips of southern hard pine stretch from front to rear and from side to side, where the ends of the ceiling are polygonal in shape. A parabolic sounding board arches from the east wall for acoustical purposes, thereby enhancing the words of the preacher or the choir from the raised platform to the assembled audience. The floor of the Auditorium is wood with cocoa matting in the aisles, and hanging light bulbs span the seven 161 foot main wood arches, the crow foot arches in the east end and the smaller arches in the west end of the hanging ceiling.

This is probably the first interior photo of the 1894 Auditorium, looking to the west.

At the official dedication ceremonies for the Auditorium, on July 1, 1894, it was evident that this building was truly a remarkable achievement for its time. During America's religious revival times, the pastoral scene of an auditorium/preacher's stand surrounded by a ring of white tents was often repeated at the more than 2,500 known camp meetings. It is from this tradition that Ocean Grove would grow to earn the unofficial title of "Queen of the Camp Meetings."

A 2010 photo – looking northwest from the gallery – shows the parabolic ceiling and the new Echo Gallery organ (located center rear).

Chapter Two

OTHER AUDITORIUMS AND OPEN-AIR BUILDINGS

One major problem in building the OGCMA Auditorium was the design of a large open space to accommodate 10,000 people at an affordable cost. New construction technologies were emerging in the building industry which would solve this problem. While the 1876 Centennial Exhibit buildings in Philadelphia and the Columbian Exposition in Chicago in 1893 set standards for open areas, the cost for such structures was beyond reach for almost all organizations. However, the growth in size of railroad terminals, bridges and armories developed the expertise for the safe and economic construction of such structures. By 1890, iron and steel-framed buildings were replacing buildings of brick, stone and wooden beams. The development of iron and steel-frame structures, the invention of electric power distribution systems, light bulbs, and elevators allowed buildings to reach 10 to 15 stories, beginning the skyscraper era.

Another concern of the twenty-six Trustees of the Camp Meeting Association was the functional design of a new structure. It was suggested that a committee visit other camp meetings and evaluate large auditoriums to avoid potential design errors. Sites included the Chautauqua Assembly in western New York State, Glen Echo near Washington, D.C., the Mormon Tabernacle at Salt Lake City, Utah, and others in Kansas, Minnesota, and Ohio. Many of these places were familiar to the Ocean Grove Trustees as some had participated in Holiness meetings at these camps. There is a short mention in the *Ocean Grove Record* of Rev. Stokes visiting Salt Lake City.

It is important for the reader to compare the 1894 Ocean Grove Auditorium to other large buildings of the late nineteenth century. The following are descriptions of two structures that are comparable, the Tabernacle at Salt Lake City and the Amphitheater at the Chautauqua Lake Camp Meeting.

Mormon Tabernacle, Salt Lake City, Utah

Construction of the Mormon Tabernacle began in 1863 and was completed in 1867. The Tabernacle is approximately 250 feet long by 150 feet wide, with a vaulted ceiling height of 80 feet. A U-shaped gallery was added to the floor plan in 1870, increasing the seating capacity to 8,000.

The exterior of the Mormon Tabernacle has a tortoise shell shaped roof, now with an aluminum metal cover.

Timbers were connected by round wooden pegs with rawhide lashings to hold the beams in place. Some rawhide thongs are still visible.

Brigham Young, President of the Latter Day Saints Church, provided the general concept of the oval-shaped Tabernacle, which from the outside resembles a smooth tortoise shell.

The design of the building was by William H. Folsom (supporting sandstone piers) and Henry Grow (domed roof), a civil engineer.

The vaulted ceiling and roof is credited to Grow, from his bridge-building experience with the Remington lattice truss. The Tabernacle arched trusses are constructed of pine timbers, each 2½ by 11½ inches, secured at joints with two-inch round wood pegs and initially lashed with rawhide thongs which are still in place at intermediate points. Two pairs of these timbers run parallel to form each chord. The pegs at each truss joint, therefore, run through six timbers, a total thickness of approximately 15 inches. This feature of construction has given rise to a popular idea that the Tabernacle was built "without a single nail," which is far from the truth. Nails were made and used for the shingles, flooring, stairs, etc. The original wood roof shingles were replaced in 1910 with sheet aluminum.

The 44 sandstone piers, columns acting as supports for the wooden roof trusses, project from the exterior wall at intervals of about 14 feet. The effect is reminiscent of buttresses projecting from a curtain wall, as in early Gothic cathedrals. Large double-hung windows, over eleven feet wide, are between each pier. The straight side walls terminate in semi-circular end walls. At the curved ends the sash and mullions follow the curvature of the wall.

In the interior of the Tabernacle, the benches of Engelmann spruce wood were hand painted to resemble oak planks, while the support columns were covered with wood designed to look like Tennessee marble. The ceiling is plaster mixed with cattle hair to give it greater strength.

Interior view of the Mormon Tabernacle, showing the ceiling curve, lighting and gallery.

Interior view of curved walls with a stairway to the gallery.

The Tabernacle is illuminated by recessed lights around the balcony, wall light fixtures underneath the gallery, and several large hanging chandeliers in the center.

The acoustics in the elliptical interior are remarkable, with the drop of a dime on a wooden bench audible throughout the entire space. The original organ was made by Joseph H. Ridges and consisted of over 700 pipes. The current organ is a 5 manual, 11,623 pipes, 206 rank Aeolian-Skinner, with the instantly recognizable original tall wooden central pipes. The Tabernacle was the first home of the 375 voice Mormon Tabernacle Choir. The Choir is now housed in a new auditorium that seats 21,600.

A post card view of the partially completed interior dome illustrates the age-old scaffolding method of roof construction. The Tabernacle is considered by many to be one of the architectural masterpieces of the United States, if not of the world, and is open year round.

While the Tabernacle was originally intended exclusively for religious purposes, as the need for a large space for secular functions became apparent, the structure began to serve both activities. The first major personality to appear in the Tabernacle was Adelina Patti, on April 1, 1884. She was followed by such performers as Nellie Zelba, Ernestine Schumann-Heink, Lili Pons, John Charles Thomas, John Philip Sousa, Vladimir Horowitz, Marian Anderson and many others, including noted lecturers and world personalities such as Shirley Temple and Helen Keller. With the exception of Calvin Coolidge, most Presidents since 1900 have spoken at the Tabernacle.

Sketch of the scaffolding necessary to construct the wooden trusses at the Mormon Tabernacle. Resembling a large skeleton, it took four years to complete the structure (1863-1867).

Chautauqua Assembly, Chautauqua, New York

Although there were differences in philosophies between Ocean Grove and Chautauqua, both began as Methodist camp meeting grounds. Ocean Grove stressed Religion, Renewal and Recreation while Chautauqua emphasized Education, Religion and the Arts. Both attracted large numbers of individuals and families, and neither would allow spirits or liquor on the camp grounds.

Engraving (1879) of the interior of the Chautauqua Amphitheater. The floor is now a combination of wood around the platform and cement on the slope.

Like Ocean Grove, the first meetings at Chautauqua in 1874 were held in a wooded area with some 2,000 people gathered in a semi-circle around a preacher's stand along the Chautauqua Lake shore. In 1877, the assemblage was moved to a large tent (Tabernacle) at the top of the lake bluff. Later, in 1879 a large earthen bowl – or Amphitheater - was created from one of the ravines that were present on the bluff.

The building committee for the new Amphitheater consisted of Lewis Miller, President and Founder, Secretary W.A. Duncan, Wm. Thomas, Esq., and architect Ellis G. Hall. The Amphitheater was covered by a roof supported by wooden pillars. The size of this open-air shed structure was 155 feet in length by 160 feet in width, or 24,800 square feet. At the lower end of the sloping bowl was the speaker's lectern and choir platform, seating 350 singers. Some 5,000 individuals sat on stiff-backed benches. The cost for this initial structure was $4,500.

In 1893, the Amphitheater was enlarged to 185 feet in length, or 29,600 square feet. The seating capacity increased to 6,000. The numerous wooden pillars that blocked the views of many were removed by the installation of steel truss beams and steel side posts. The speaker/choir platform was further enlarged to accommodate 500 persons. To the rear of the platform was added a large reception area, several offices, new lighting and music preparation rooms. The total cost of this reconstruction was reported at approximately $26,000.

There are no walls to the open-air Amphitheater except for canvas drops. In the winter time, snow drifts can be observed covering some rows of seats. The wooden ceiling is a low parabolic arch with hanging lights. The truss space between the interior parabolic wooden ceiling and the roof provides

Replacement of the wooden pillars with steel posts increased the visibility of the center stage for the audience. The American flag, choir seating and organ arrangement are similar to those at Ocean Grove.

some noise reduction, particularly during periods of heavy summer rainstorms. The acoustic properties of the Amphitheater are considered "exceptionally fine." In 1907, a gift of $40,000 from the Massey family provided for a new 5,000 pipe organ from the Warren Organ Company of Woodstock, Ontario. This was installed behind the semi-circle of choir seats. As in Ocean Grove, the Chautauqua Amphitheater is open only in the summer.

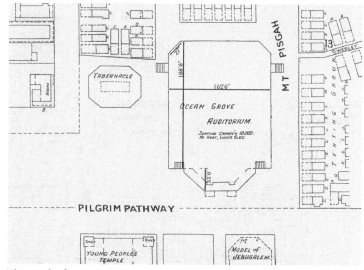

This early fire insurance map (n.d.) places the Auditorium in relation to surrounding buildings, including the tents and Tabernacle. The two exterior staircases extend straight out from the building.

The following provides additional comparisons of late nineteenth century public spaces:

1. **The Auditorium Building of Roosevelt University, Chicago, IL, 1889,** design by Sullivan and Adler. Seating capacity 4,200 – 6,000; arches with recessed lighting, theatre is trumpet-shaped for near perfect acoustics, year round ventilation system, plaster ceiling.

2. **Madison Square Garden, New York, NY, 1889-90,** designed by Stanford White. Oval shaped arena, seating capacity about 8,000 people with room for another 6,000 people standing, ceiling of exposed Pratt trusses, and 186 foot span with hundreds of incandescent lights mounted on overhead arches. (Editor's note: this building was demolished in 1925 for a new Madison Square Garden.)

3. **Thirteenth Regiment Armory, Brooklyn, NY, 1893**. Iron framework construction for the drill hall by Milliken Brothers, Brooklyn, NY. Span 196 feet; 12 arches. First use of gin poles for erecting arches.

4. **Examples of Railroad Train Sheds Include:**
   Grand Central I, New York, 1869-71. Span 200 feet; height 100 feet; arched lattice truss
   Broad Street Station I, Philadelphia, 1881-1882. Span 160 feet; pointed arched rib.
   Jersey City, Pennsylvania Station, 1888. Span 252 feet; height 86 feet; three-hinged arched lattice rib.
   Reading Terminal, Philadelphia, 1891-93. Span 267 feet; height 88 feet; three-centered pointed-arch roof 559 feet long.

5. **Mormon Tabernacle, Salt Lake City, Utah, 1863-1867**. Span 150 feet; height 80 feet; Remington truss.

6. **Chautauqua Amphitheater, Chautauqua, NY, 1893**. Span 160 feet; height 34 feet at the bottom of the slope; truss arch with support columns.

7. **Ocean Grove Camp Meeting Auditorium, Ocean Grove, NJ, 1894**. Span 161 feet; height 55 feet, three-section arch.

Looking out from the pulpit, this interior photo of the third auditorium is from a stereo-optic. The park-bench settees would eventually be utilized in the balcony of the new building. Notice the line of tents in the background.

Exterior of the third auditorium; janitors building on right. Even the wren's bird house (right foreground) was removed to make room for the new building. The hand-written date of 1892 is incorrect; this building was torn down in October 1893.

Chapter Three

A Journey of Faith: Raising of Funds

As Ocean Grove's attendance grew after 1869, so did its need for larger facilities. The Camp Meeting desperately needed a larger Auditorium, having rapidly outgrown three smaller structures in only 25 years. Roughly 350,000 people visited Ocean Grove during the summer of 1892. The third Auditorium seated only 4200, in a space of 136 feet by 146 feet, with another 1000-1500 people left standing or sitting on the grounds outside.

As early as 1883, Stokes began to urge that a fourth and larger auditorium was necessary to accommodate the escalating crowds of worshipers. Stokes persisted in his dream for ten years, with his focus on having a new facility in place by 1894, which was the Twenty-Fifth Silver Anniversary of the founding of the Camp Meeting.

The raising of extra funds for a new auditorium was a challenge. The development and operation costs of the Camp Meeting and its programs were increasing with each season, and the country was experiencing economic hard times in the late 1880s. Furthermore, the Trustees passed a resolution as a general guide that two-thirds of the required funds must be subscribed before any changes to the existing auditorium could begin. Some donations were received in the form of one-hundred dollar gold coins and other pledges. The average weekly pay for a workman in the 1890s was about $3 a week. The dilemma was how to raise $45,000 - $50,000 in a short time without draining the Camp Meeting's generous donors and still leave the Association able to pay all annual operating costs after payments to the contractors for the new auditorium.

The following excerpts from the 1892-1894 Annual Reports of the Camp Meeting deal directly with issues of funding a new auditorium. Originally the words of Ellwood Stokes, but now presented in a narrative form, one can witness Stokes' powerful statements of belief and faith that this project could be accomplished to the glory of God - and it was.

Stokes Proposes Larger Auditorium - Trustees are Unsure

Stokes' campaign for a permanent house of worship was carefully calculated, even before architectural plans were solicited or one dollar was raised. As the Camp Meeting approached its twenty-fifth anniversary, he began impressing his vision on those around him, both on the street and in his writings.

One compelling reason for a new Auditorium, he argued in the 1892 Annual Report, was that the "summer multitudes" in Ocean Grove far outnumbered the available seats. "If one-half should demand seats for the public service, we should be utterly unable to furnish them," Stokes warns. "'More room' is the public cry." Stokes' primary concern was that to not supply seats was to have "our people drift from us." And, he reminded the trustees, "many of our people sit on these hard and uncomfortable seats from six to eight hours in a single day!" Providing superior accommodations for worship was Ocean Grove's "peculiar work." "For this we were raised up, organized, and for this we stand before the church and the world, most solemnly committed," Stokes proclaimed. "In this work, and nowhere else, lies our special strength," he told them, adding, "we must provide…or we (will) fall from our position of eminence we may have gained to the level of other places, losing the divine prestige which has been given us of God."

Choosing his words carefully, Stokes respectfully suggested a design for a new building, and encouraged the trustees to solicit approved plans. The building "will seat, by actual measurement, at least 10,000 persons, more if possible," Stokes said. With a roof of iron, concave or tortoise-shell shaped, thereby creating a "perfect sounding board," the building could feature "complete acoustic properties, bringing the whole audience of 10,000 or more in pleasant reach by an ordinary voice." Stokes also suggested proper methods of ventilation and space for a choir "at least 500 strong."

To dream of the Auditorium was admirable; to raise the money required Stokes' sheer determination and unwavering faith. "It can be done!" he urged. "Are there not among our many thousands of friends, twenty-five who will give $1000 each and as many more who will give $500? Besides these," he added, "vast multitudes of others will give $100, $50, $25, $10, $5, $1, etc." Stokes claimed that two gentlemen, without solicitation, already agreed to give $1000, and others were ready to do the same. He recommended that the trustees find friends of Ocean Grove in neighboring cities and towns to assist in the raising of funds. "No better missionary work for immediate results, than to help build this Auditorium," he encouraged them.

Not about to let any nay-sayers off the hook, Stokes pushed the trustees in the summer of 1892. "What action, if any, must be decided before the adjournment of this Annual Meeting?" he asks. "Without an absolute decree at this meeting, we shall lose our opportunity. I have now, and have had for the last three years, a profound conviction, that this New Auditorium should be built, and ready for occupancy, by the summer of 1894, our silver wedding year." Stokes warned the trustees that to ignore the wave of current interest in building a larger facility would be to lose the opportunity. He appealed to any doubters: "God has committed to us a great work, the magnitude of which none of us fully comprehend. It is to lift all Christian people to a higher plane of the religious life – to enthuse the church of all denominations, with highest and holiest ambitions – to educate in the best methods of bringing sinners to the cross, to save men, and to bless the world."

As Stokes called upon the trustees to review Ocean Grove's latest financial statement and the feasibility of fund raising, Stokes implored them to carry the torch. "The day of small things with us is past. The day of a great opportunity has come," he told them. "For a long time, I have carried the burden of this New Auditorium. I bend beneath its weight. Will you, by your decided action this day, help me bear it?"

Stokes was so thoroughly convinced of this endeavor that he predicted the Camp Meeting could raise two-thirds of the cost by the following year. "Plan strongly for a New Auditorium Day, Sabbath, July 30, 1893," he stated. "All that is needed to

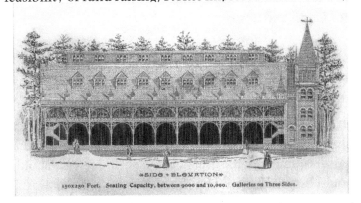

SIDE ELEVATION
150x250 Feet. Seating Capacity, between 9000 and 10,000. Galleries on Three Sides.

This sketch is of a proposed auditorium 150 by 250 feet in size with a ground floor and gallery capable of seating between 9,500-10,000 people. There are nine large openings along the side with gallery stairs at both ends. Ventilation is provided by nine dormers spread midway along the roof with Clerestory windows at the roof peak.

do this is a steady faith, and holy enthusiasm. These will remove mountains. It can be done by us, for in addition to faith and a holy enthusiasm, God has given us the confidence of the people."

Stokes Plans a "New Auditorium Day" to Solicit Funds

Stokes presentation to the Trustees in October 11, 1892 was "received with silent courtesy." The country was in the midst of a financial crisis, with no end in sight, and the "thought entertained by the majority was, that in view of the greatness of the work, and the financial depression prevailing…the period was not auspicious for such an undertaking." Although greatly disheartened, Stokes received permission to pursue plans and obtain an approximate cost of a new building and to report at an adjourned meeting of the Association in December 1892.

At the Trustees meeting on December 22, 1892, a local architect, W. H. Carman, Esq., submitted a sample sketch of an auditorium for the Trustees to consider. The building measured 150 feet by 250 feet in size, with a seating capacity between 9,000 and 10,000 people. The cost was estimated at $50,000, but other estimates ranged from $60,000 and $80,000. The Trustees found the cost to be "beyond the grasp of the most enthusiastic hope." Not to be deterred, Stokes pressed for some action before the meeting adjourned. There was, he felt, "sufficient basis that a building could be erected which would come within the possibility of an intelligent and united Christian effort." The Trustees approved further investigation, and if sufficient data for action could be obtained to warrant further progress, a special session of the Association would be called.

OCEAN GROVE, N. J., July 13, 1893.

DEAR FRIEND:

Believing you such, we thus address you.

Our present Auditorium has done a work and made a history, equaled by few structures of its age in this or any other country.

Thousands have here, for the first time, accepted Christ as a Saviour, and countless other thousands have been quickened to a better life.

This structure having passed through various changes is now twenty-four years old.

We need a *new one!* Not for human show or glory, but for greater capacity, and increased conveniences.

Next summer, 1894, will be our "SILVER WEDDING." This fall, winter and spring will therefore, be the time to build, if we are to enter our new edifice on our Silver Wedding anniversary.

We aim to accommodate 10,000 people. We have had different plans, and estimates. Some are too costly. These now under consideration (see outside of this card), will cost $50,000, seated with comfortable chairs.

Such a building, for obvious reasons, can be built only by public subscriptions.

We are satisfied that you will help us. The many pleasant days spent here, and the intellectual and spiritual benefits received by yourself, children or friends will prompt this.

This whole Ocean Grove work is missionary, and money for this structure, will be a missionary investment, yielding immediate returns.

The building of this new structure will broaden and give greater permanency to this place, and by that much increase the value of property.

Thus far, we have not solicited subscriptions, but pledges have been quite largely volunteered.

It now looks as if we should receive nearly, or quite one-third of the whole cost in *one thousand dollar* subscriptions. Perhaps not, but still we hope. After these large subscriptions will come the hardest of the work. But faith and united effort will bring success.

August 13, 1893, has been set apart as *New Auditorium Day.* Chaplain McCabe will preach at 10.30 A. M., and the people will have an opportunity to assist in this great work.

If you cannot be present, send your pledge by mail. The money can be paid in three installments, October and December, 1893 and February, 1894.

Speak a kind word, pray for and help us all you can. This work will bless the ages after we are gone.

On behalf of the Association,

E. H. STOKES, *President.*

A card from July 1893 contains a plea from Rev. Stokes for Ocean Grovers to prepare for a "New Auditorium Day." Stokes handed them out to everyone he saw on the street, laying the seeds for Fundraising. The flip side of the card featured the proposed sketch for an Auditorium.

At the next semi-annual meeting, May 1893, and after a careful examination of the whole subject, consent was given to go forward and test the willingness of the people to contribute the amount of $50,000, the approximate cost figure.

A jubilant Stokes reminded the Trustees to "plan strongly for a New Auditorium Day, Sabbath, July 31, 1893." If two-thirds of the money was committed, the building was feasible. "Vastly more improbable things have been, and are now in course of successful accomplishment," he encouraged the group.

FRONT VIEW OF PROPOSED NEW AUDITORIUM—FACING EAST.

The front three story façade is balanced by two large towers with louvers, flanking an eight panel rose window. Two horizontal rows of windows suggest three or four rooms on each floor. Gothic items include a matched column entrance, corner cupolas, weather vanes and miniature turrets.

The Trustees called upon the financial talents of Chaplain C. C. McCabe to coordinate the effort. Chaplain McCabe, popular for his promotion of the song *Mine Eyes Have Seen the Glory* (or *The Battle Hymn of the Republic*), was a well-known Civil War veteran and survivor of the Libby Confederate prison. But McCabe was not available for July 31 so the date was moved to August 13. The summer season loomed, and Stokes renewed his campaign with the residents. He had 90 days to convince his flock, and anyone who passed him on the street received a fund-raising card.

The Laymen's Mass Meeting – August 11, 1893

In the weeks prior to New Auditorium Day, Stokes was nervous, calling it a period of "great solicitude." "Mental conflicts arose, darkness intensified, and God seemed to hide Himself," he wrote. But hope arrived "like a sunburst on a dark night" through a proposition from an old friend, David H. Wyckoff, Esq., of Asbury Park, for a Laymen's Mass Meeting. Wyckoff suggested a meeting for Friday night, August 11, to be conducted by the laymen and for the laymen. Ministers – and trustees – were to have nothing to do with the meeting. A vast audience attended, and Wyckoff spoke enthusiastically about the possibilities of the new auditorium. Hon. James A. Bradley presided, and gave an address; other speakers included Gen. Rusling, N. E. Buchanon, A. H. DeHaven, John A. Githens and E. T. Lovatt. Excitement mounted, as Miss Emma Johnson wrote a hymn, "*There's a Call to the Faithful Soul.*" Although no collection was taken, "resolutions of high moral and financial support were unanimously and triumphantly passed." One woman gave an oil painting, which was sold for $100; another woman, who had already donated two horses, a carriage and harness, now gave a gold watch and chain, which were sold for $100. The laymen's meeting brought great relief to Stokes. "Man's extremity is God's opportunity," he said. Still, the upcoming Sabbath loomed, with the funding for a new auditorium hanging precariously in the balance.

Daniel H. Wyckoff (1829-1900) was a prominent business man with services in the paint and lumber supply. He was a Justice of the Peace as well as a member of the State Legislature. He always worked toward the improvement of Asbury Park and settled disputes without lawsuits. A strong Methodist, he called himself "The Peace Maker," and spearheaded the Layman's Meetings to create enthusiasm for a new Auditorium.

New Auditorium Day: August 13, 1893

A great disappointment occurred in town as word was received from Chaplain McCabe that, because of a family affliction, he would be unable to fulfill his engagement as coordinator of funds. And so on the Sabbath, August 13, 1893, the church service began promptly at ten o'clock, McCabe's absence from the platform quite evident and causing whispers.

A vast audience, full of the highest expectations, crowded the Auditorium. It was "a matchless day, without a cloud in the sky, and the temperature exactly right." The introductory services opened, proceeded, and closed as usual. Then President Stokes arose and read Chaplain McCabe's letter. There was a ripple of disappointment; but not a hand stirred, or foot moved. Before the audience had time to react, they were engulfed in an address from Stokes, in which "all his brain, heart and soul were concentrated, accompanied with a cyclone of Divine power received directly from the Eternal Throne."

Stokes spoke only ten minutes, but his message was powerful: "I am grieved for your sakes that Chaplain McCabe is not here; but great and good and grand as he is, he cannot have half the interest in this work that I have, or you have. He would be a stranger here, but this is your summer home, and this is the culmination of my life work. Shall we heed the plea and build? 'Hard times,' do you say? Yes, and they will be harder if we do not do more for God. 'Widow's mites,' do you say? Oh, if we could only get the widow's mites! Yes, she cast in two mites even all her living! There is as much money as ever. It belongs to God. Give a part to Him, He may take it all."

Other supporters spoke in the same convincing strain: Hon. James A. Bradley, Dr. Hanlon, and Brother C. H. Yatman.

James Adam Bradley (1830-1921) was a successful brush manufacturer in New York City who was introduced to the Jersey Shore and Ocean Grove by D. H. Brown, a Brooklyn banker and a Trustee of the OGCMA. Bradley, a converted Methodist, was so supportive of the principles of the camp meeting that he purchased for $90,000 some 500 acres of land north of Wesley Lake to Deal Lake and named it Asbury Park in honor of Francis Asbury, the earlier founder of Methodism in the US. His design of Asbury Park included park lands, land for churches, civic groups and the public library. He also applied a setback concept to the first ocean streets in Asbury Park.

By eleven o'clock, the trustees were ready for subscriptions. There were two vast blackboards placed on the platform, in full view of the people, with sums from $1 to $1,000 marked on each, both boards exactly alike, aggregating $45,000. Assisting were five secretaries and two brothers with chalk in hand, to mark off the sums as they were taken.

And so the giving commenced. Fourteen of the sixteen $1,000 donations were speedily taken. Then smaller sums, $500, $100, $50, $25, etc., came "like the rapids of Niagara, all seemingly afraid they would not get a chance to give; while people laughed, wept, clapped their hands for joy, shouted like the sound of many waters." The customary noon dinner was forgotten, and the tide of giving "swirled, dashed, and rolled" until one o'clock. At two o'clock, pledging began again in Dr. Hanlon's Bible Class, who had asked members to contribute $20,000 of the $50,000 needed to do the work. Still, while few thought the goal could be reached, the tide was slowly changing: pledge commitments were pouring in.

The generosity in giving flowed anew, right through the six o'clock Beach Meeting Service under Brother Yatman. Again at the evening service, there was another enthusiastic outpouring and demonstration at the Auditorium. When the meeting closed at ten o'clock, approximately $42,000 was subscribed for the new building. Stokes described the evening service in glowing words, "The multitudes were enthused, surprised, dazed, at what they saw, heard, and felt. In the stillness of night, which had settled down upon us, high and repeated doxologies of overflowing joy burst from the exultant thousands, and in the midst of the universal cry of hard times, seemed more like a midnight vagary than real, or a miracle of Divine Power, rather than wrought by human agents."

For the next day and for weeks to come, promise of new subscriptions continued to pour in. For days it was difficult for Stokes to pass along the streets of Ocean Grove, as he received congratulations, telegrams and letters joined to the general joy. "We do not take honor to ourselves," he told the people, "It belongs to God, and He has, and shall have it."

Last Service in the Old Building

On Sunday, September, 10, 1893, the final service was held in the old building, in the presence of a great audience, amid sighs, and sobs and tears. Services commenced at 10:00 a.m., and Stokes delivered an address, reciting the leading facts concerning the old Auditorium. In 24 years, the total numbers of services offered were 12,873, or 1½ services a day for 22 years, 365 days to the year.

OLD AUDITORIUM, 1880-1893.

The old develops new,
Like bursting buds from Aaron's withered rod,
Or a white lily from the cold black sod,
Like sweet fresh life, from the warm heart of God;
Like morning's pearly dew
On the dry grass flashing beneath the skies,
So from the old, New Auditoriums rise,
And truths evolve, Christ-hued, each a divine surprise.—

Many Ocean Grovers were very emotional about the demolition of the third Auditorium after the summer season of 1893. This brief poem, by Rev. Stokes, encouraged the people to keep faith.

As could be best estimated, the approximate numbers "converted, reclaimed, especially helped, and sanctified" during the 24 years were: Converted - 7,050; Sanctified - 4,900; Reclaimed - 4,500; Especially helped - 55,800; for a total of 72,250 persons affected by the Gospel message.

Sunday afternoon was occupied by an old-time Love Feast, admission by ticket, and the distribution of the cake and water, the symbol of mutual friendship and Christian love. Stokes reported that "the testimonies of tenderness and love for the old time-honored edifice were many and tearful." The evening was taken up with an evangelistic service, led by Rev. C. H. Yatman, who delivered a brief address, followed by Stokes, W. H. Skirm, Dr. Hanlon, A. H. DeHaven, and E. T. Lovatt. Then Stokes, after a closing prayer, the last ever offered there, pronounced the final benediction, "in the name of the Father, Son, and Holy Ghost," the bell striking three times.

With $42,600 pledged or in hand from summer 1893, Stokes had a mere nine months to deliver a new facility to the believers. There would be no slow winter season for him. He began immediately advertising for construction bids, and tearing down of the present structure. There was no turning back once the old Auditorium was dismantled.

"Request for Proposal" for designs for a new Auditorium appeared in various newspapers in New Jersey, New York and Pennsylvania.

Ocean Grove's Silver Anniversary Monument:
"The Largest and Finest Evangelical Audience Room in the Known World"

It is now July 1, 1894, and after 92 days of construction the new Auditorium was officially open. Rev. E. H. Stokes gave the first sermon (50 minutes in length) to a full house, setting forth the uses and goals of this new structure and of the Ocean Grove Camp Meeting. Attending the service that morning was 21-year old William Milligan. The following account is taken directly from his personal journal:

> This morning Jessie and I attended the opening service in the New Auditorium. Before this, however, we attended the first Young People's Meeting of the season which was held in the Temple under the leadership of Mr. Chas. H. Yatman, the well-known and greatly beloved evangelist who made the Young People's Meetings of Ocean Grove what they are.
>
> The New Auditorium is a magnificent structure. I liked it much better than I did last night. It is arranged that the sides can be slid up and sideways making it to appear as the old auditorium, which had no walls at all. There is one gallery running around the entire sides of the building and an arched roof about one hundred feet above the floor. The floor rises from the platform making it possible for all to see who speaks easily. Over the platform on the wall are the words "Holiness to the Lord" in incandescent lamps, and on the wall which is shaped like a section of an octagon are also the words "Glory to God in the highest and on Earth, Peace, and Good Will toward Men" in large lettering.
>
> The platform will seat over one hundred persons while the Auditorium will seat ten thousand persons. This is the largest building used for evangelical purposes in the United States and probably in the World. There were probably six thousand at this morning's service. The galleries are marvels of immensity, being larger than two or three churches like St. James in New York City. The furniture is of light colored wood as is the woodwork. This gives the place a very cherry [sic] look. There is a fine antique oak organ, a small one seeming for so large a hall, but it amply fills the room with its rich melodies. It is made so that it can either be pumped by a bellows worked by a person standing at the side or by foot power.
>
> The desk over which so many noted and venerable divines, many of whom have gone to their reward, have preached, would not be parted with, but has been painted a pure white and decorated rich gold making it a beautiful thing to look upon. The entire floor space of the building is covered with cocoa matting. There is not a pillar in the hall except those, which support the galleries. The span of the roof is immense. There are four exits and entrances for the gallery, the main floor being almost as open as the old building. If concerts or exhibitions of stereopticon pictures, etc., are to be given and admission fees charged, this building can be closed and be as serviceable as any other. This is also convenient late in the season when it is cool outdoors and also in wet and windy weather. I cannot describe the

feeling of awe and admiration which took possession of men on beholding the interior of this building and the more I look upon the exterior, the more I like it. The front façade is very imposing. There is a tower, which rises about one hundred and thirty feet in the air, and two smaller ones on each end.

Rev. Dr. Ellwood H. Stokes, president of the Ocean Grove Camp Meeting Association, delivered the opening sermon or rather address welcoming all the people to the hospitality of the place. The address was very impressive indeed coming as it did from the lips of the man who has been the ruling spirit of this place from its inception and who in a large measure has been the means of making Ocean Grove what it is. He brought up many reminiscences and spoke often of the future of this great building, giving many suggestions and thoughts which were very wise.

Many groups clamored to use the new facility, and the 1894 summer program was full. Besides the weekly Sunday worship services, programs included the W.C.T.U. (Women's Christian Temperance Union) of New Jersey, Sunday School Assemblies, the National Education Convention, Stereopticon views and lectures, concerts, King's Daughters' Day, African M.E. Church Jubilee, and others.

Dedication of the New Auditorium – August 9-12, 1894

The new Auditorium dedication ceremonies were scheduled for Thursday, August 9 to Sabbath, August 12 with the annual camp meeting beginning on Monday, August 20 to August 30. But even as visitors poured into the new Auditorium during the month of July 1894, Stokes' heart was heavy with a burden: he still needed additional funds to cover all the bills for the Auditorium.

Once again, David Wyckoff, of Asbury Park, was inspired to call a Laymen's Meeting for August 6 at 8 p.m., similar to the one held the previous year, "of the laity, by the laity, and for the laity." At both these meetings, Hon. James A. Bradley presided, and large numbers of prominent gentlemen from both Asbury Park and Ocean Grove gave brief addresses. High enthusiasm prevailed, and the results of both were very helpful in enabling the Camp Meeting to reach the desirable financial end. The musical arrangements, under the direction of Prof. John Sweeney, included the Park Sisters and others. Stokes exclaims in the Annual Report, "It was a great meeting, great in numbers, great in enthusiasm, great in its influence for good, and great in the satisfaction which it gave to all, and all have our profoundest thanks."

For the dedication ceremonies of the new Auditorium, Stokes extended personal invitations to the entire 18-member Board of Bishops of the Methodist Episcopal Church. For most, issues of time, extreme travel distance and other prevailing church commitments were expressed via regrets, but three bishops accepted the invitation: Bishop Thomas Bowman, of St. Louis, Missouri (Senior Bishop); Bishop John M. Walden, of Cincinnati, Ohio, and Bishop Charles H. Fowler, of Minneapolis, Minnesota. Added to these guests were Chaplain McCabe, Corresponding Secretary of the Parent Missionary Society, Methodist Episcopal Church; Dr. A. J. Palmer, of New York, and Rev. C. E. Mandeville, D.D., of Chicago. Following the Sunday evening sermon, Bishop Bowman, assisted by all the Bishops and other ministers present, would formally dedicate the house to the service and worship of Almighty God.

Four days of programs and services were planned, beginning on Thursday morning, August 9, and running through Sunday evening, August 12. Stokes was ecstatic with the services, reporting that the sermons by the Bishops "were each crowning summits of their own, such as we rarely reach," and the "lectures by the trio of peerless lecturers was another range of patriotic culminations – great cyclonic

Participants in New Auditorinm Dedicatory Services, August 9–12, 1894.

Bishop CHAS. H. FOWLER.   Bishop JOHN M. WALDEN.
Bishop THOS. BOWMAN.
Rev. A. J. PALMER, D. D.   Chaplain C. C. McCABE.

This photo collage shows those who participated in the opening ceremonies. The lower right corner is the popular Rev. Charles Caldwell McCabe (1836-1906), who served as a Chaplain in the Civil War. He was very successful as a fund raiser for the Methodist Church and used his baritone voice for such causes. Later, he was chosen as a Bishop in the Methodist Church. At the dedication services in the new Auditorium, McCabe preached about "The Bright Side of Life at Libby Prison," where he nearly died from the unsanitary prison conditions.

sweeps of resistless eloquence, before which the heart and intellect bowed like the sturdy oaks and cedars in tempest's march."

Particularly moving was the service led by Chaplain C. C. McCabe, a Civil War veteran and a survivor of the Libby Confederate prison. His "sermons moved the deepest emotions of the soul, and the lectures kindled the flames of the loftiest patriotism." As veterans of the Civil War marched into the new Auditorium "with their tattered flags and ensigns, some with empty sleeves and limping steps, to occupy seats reserved for them in the front," the whole assembly of ten thousand people rose, *en masse*, as cheer after cheer resounded through the vast enclosure, and the enthusiasm knew no bounds.

Sunday morning August 12 arrived; it was not rainy, yet not particularly clear. "All things work together for good to them that love God," Stokes reminded himself as he walked to the new Auditorium, for in the pocket of his suit was an appeal for more money: he still needed $26,000 to pay off all the Auditorium bills. At 10 o'clock, the great house was full and the services commenced. Songs melted the heart, and a prayer by Dr. Alday "touched the throne." Stokes approached the pulpit, and began his emotional petition:

> *For the past twenty-five years I have carried this great enterprise on my soul. For the past five years the ideal of this new Auditorium has been constantly before my mind. It is now a vast dream realized. I call it vast not simply because of the extent of the wall, but more especially with reference to its exalted aims to reach the remotest parts of the earth, and bring the world, too long in rebellion against God, in humble submission to his feet.*
>
> *In its management, this great interest is denominational; in its practical workings it is vastly greater than a denomination, or creed or ecclesiastical system, for it takes in all which have Christ for their Central Sun, and focusing the light and heat of each, until all, aglow with the hallowed fire, shall melt and mould our common humanity into the image of God.*

We want to enthuse the world with the divine ambition of a better life – to lift man to a loftier plane – to lead him to mountain summits of divinest privilege – to show the immensities of present opportunities – to move all hearts, to move all churches – to move the work heavenward.

Today I address all the denominations. For twenty-five years we have tried to help you. You have gone to your homes to help your own people. You have helped them with help you obtained here. I am glad of it. Revivals have followed in the local churches. New forces have been awakened, new churches have been built, and the kingdom of God has been extended. One year ago you so helped us as to make the erection of this vast edifice possible.

It stands before us to-day like a great silent vision, almost too ethereal to be of earth, something let down from heaven, until we feel that the Tabernacle of God is with men.

There is just one additional step to be taken, and this great Temple, completed and emancipated from all earthly claims, shall stand, the home of gladness, not to narrow men, but Amazon-like to broaden them out to the great sea of God's infinite and eternal love.

Rev. Ellwood Stokes, first president of the Camp Meeting Association.

O, house of God! What a mission is thine – to stand forth for long centuries in doing good.

I said, I have carried this enterprise for the quarter of a century. I bend a little with the weight. The burden is too heavy. Will each one of you lift a little from my shoulders? If a man by the wayside was crushed beneath his burden, you would help him, would you not? There is one other step to raise, just one, and we reach the summit of this Endeavour. But I cannot raise that step without help. Take my hand, brothers, and help me up, will you? I am in a pit, twenty-six thousand dollars deep, won't you help me out? There are twenty-six thousand fetters on this noble building. Shall this be emancipation day and liberty be proclaimed through all the land, then the joy bells of ten thousand hearts shall out-throb the clang of the old independence bell in Philadelphia, a hundred years ago? It can be done! If we could raise $41,000 a year ago, simply in hope of what might be, can we not raise $26,000 in the great throbbing joy of what we now see? We can; and the ear of my faith hears the clang of the last fetter falling to the earth.

To this heartfelt appeal, others added earnest and eloquent words: Bishop Bowman, Senator Bradley, Dr. Hanlon, and Rev. Yatman. At 11 a.m., the blackboards were again unveiled on the stage, the Secretaries were at the tables, and Mr. Lovatt, Gen. Patterson, and others were in their places to mark off the sums announced. For two hours, it was a long, steady, but enthusiastic march upward, and by 1:00 p.m., $13,000 of the $26,000, was subscribed. After a lunch break, members of Dr. Hanlon's early afternoon Bible Class pledged another $1,000. Yet Stokes was still $12,000 short, with only one service remaining for the dedicatory weekend.

No one saw just how that sum could be reached, but "man's extremity is God's opportunity." Later, at 4:00 in the afternoon, an informal gathering of a few friends was held in the President's room. Listening attentively to the concerns of those meeting, a gentleman from Yonkers, New York, (and a stranger to most) queried Stokes, "You need $12,000?" "Yes," replied Stokes. "Then divide it into three blocks, $4,000 each; I will give one-quarter of the first block, one-third of the second block, and one-half of the last block, if the several remainders shall be taken by the congregation."

This generous and unexpected challenge made by John E. Andrus was, in the words of Stokes, like "a sun burst on an Egyptian night." By the evening service, the congregation was buzzing with excitement. The challenge was presented to the

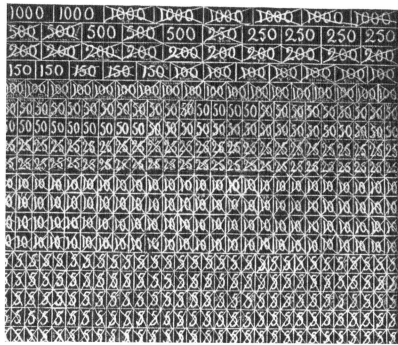

A facsimile of one of the fund raising black boards that displayed the pledge amounts from $1 to $1,000. Congregants opened their hearts and purses at the two fund raising services, August 13, 1893, and August 12, 1894, to meet the monetary goals.

immense audience, and "thrilled every heart with hope and gladness." Bishop Fowler preached with a vengeance, "a masterly effort." The Bishops, Presiding Elders, Ministers of the rank and file, laymen and general solicitors worked the congregation. Eight thousand dollars were raised! The last block of $4,000 was announced amid high inspirations. Again John Andrus, who had made

John E. Andrus of Yonkers, NY, presented a challenge grant of $6,000 dollars to Rev. Stokes on Sunday afternoon, August 12, 1894. By 10:45 p.m. that night, the faithful delivered the remaining funds.

the original block proposition, stepped in and announced, "I will give $250 for each one of my children, and I have eight of them." At this declaration of $2000 more, enthusiasm over-leaped all barriers, submerging all. As Stokes said, "The remaining part of the mountain rise was comparatively an easy ascent;" and at 10:45 p.m. the last dollar and the summit were reached.

All faces were wreathed in smiles, or flushed with exultant joy – hands were shaken, congratulations extended, cornets, and trombones, glad songs, doxologies and *"Blow ye the trumpet blow,"* mingled together in orderly and sublime confusion. In the midst of these intense emotions, Stokes once more addressed the congregation:

From the deepest depths of my overburdened heart, I thank every body, the child that gave the penny, the widow with her mites, the nickels, the dimes, the quarters, the halves, the dollars, tens, hundreds, thousands, up to our last great deliverer, Mr. Andrus, who gave his $4,333.33!

May the divine All-Father send his gracious benedictions upon all, near and far, men, women, and children, and fill this new Temple with the highest glory of Him.

Then Bishop Bowman, aided by Bishops Walden and Fowler, the ministers and the whole vast multitude, which had remained present up to the late hour, joined in the beautifully solemn ritual, which set apart this "divinely Monumental Temple," to the service and worship of Almighty God. After which Professor John Sweeney, the choir and all the great host, sang – in the loftiest tones of holy triumph: "Glory be to the Father, and to the Son, and to the Holy Ghost. As it was in the beginning, is now, and ever shall be, world without end. Amen." And the dedicatory services for the new Auditorium were at an end.

Old Auditorium,

So thy great works we sum,

And now, adieu;

Our bosoms sadly swell,

Yet thy expiring knell,

New joys our hearts impel:

Faith sees the new!

EHS

Chapter Four

Iron-Work Contract

On Monday, August 14, 1893, immediately following New Auditorium Day and the commitment of $42,500 to the cause, Stokes issued a call for construction bids through the public newspapers in Philadelphia, New York and New Jersey. The suggested size for designs was given as 150 feet by 250 feet, to accommodate 10,000 people. By mid-September, the Camp Meeting received 15 different plans and estimates from such noted companies as the Berlin Iron Bridge Company, and the Wrought Iron Bridge Company of New York.

A committee of six trustees evaluated the plans for both practicality and financial costs. The Committee consisted of D. H. Brown, treasurer, George W. Evans, Wm. H. Kirm, A. H. DeHaven, T. J. Preston and E. H. Stokes as chairman. A second round evaluating four of the 15 plans was held on October 10, 1893. The committee recommended the plans of New York architect Frederick T. Camp, and all accepted the choice "as from above." Some thirty or more formal meetings were held by the committee in order to simplify, adjust or amplify the contracts for the building. Camp had just 45 days to generate the plans for the iron and woodwork, and selected the noted iron and steel contractors Milliken Brothers of Brooklyn to build the framework.

Milliken Brothers

The Milliken Brothers firm was founded by Edward Milliken (1863-1906) and Foster Milliken (1865-1945) in Brooklyn, NY, in 1889. Their father, Samuel Milliken (1820-1898) was in the iron and steel contracting business with such firms as Logan Iron Furnace, Howard Furnace, Valentine & Thomas and the Phoenix Iron Works. In 1889, Samuel's firm of Milliken, Smith and Company dissolved, but his two sons continued for a while as agents of the Phoenix Iron Works through the new company, Milliken Brothers. The business prospered to the extent that Milliken Brothers had two small plants in Brooklyn to supply their own iron and steel products for clients throughout the United States as well as the world.

The Milliken Brothers' Brooklyn plants, employing 600 people, could not meet the demands for building materials, and in 1901-1903 a 175-acre site was purchased on the west shore of Staten Island. This location was ideal, because it provided fast transportation access to Newark Bay, the 21-foot deep Van Name Channel, and the New York Transit and Terminal Company Railroad. With a work force increased to 1400 workers, Milliken Brothers was able to bid on large iron supply contracts in the New York City area and developed a reputation as a reliable supplier of material from its steel mill. Other noted contracts included sugar mills in Cuba and Hawaii, Palace of Fine Arts in Mexico City, and the Rio Grande Railroad Bridge with a center arch of 450 feet in Costa Rica. Notable buildings in New York City include the New York Clearing House, Hotel Majestic, the 69th Street Armory, the

Singer Building, and the Pennsylvania Railroad Station, and in New Jersey, the Higginsville Bridge in Somerset County. Elsewhere in the United States, Milliken Brothers supplied the steel for the Wainwright Building in St. Louis, Missouri.

The Milliken Brothers firm had the expertise to design iron trusses for the Ocean Grove Auditorium, having manufactured other frame-works of similar size. In 1893, Milliken Brothers had completed the framework on the Thirteenth Regiment Armory, located between Lewis and Sumner Streets in Brooklyn, NY. This Armory drill hall was about 280 feet in length by 196 feet in width without any intermediate supports.

Up to this time, the assembly of a wide truss arch was a simple but slow procedure based on the design and precision of the connection points between the individual parts

The first use (1893) of gin poles by Milliken Brothers at the 13th Regiment Armory in Brooklyn, NY.

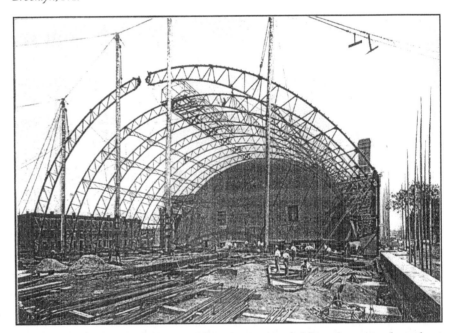

Here is a photo of the center section of the truss – suspended from the mast poles – about to be connected in midair to the other sections by Milliken workers.

of the arch. A scaffold would be constructed up to the underside of the proposed truss. The parts of the truss were then laid on the scaffolding and connected with rivets and bolts. The scaffolding would then be enlarged to the next truss. Connecting cross beams and lattices between the trusses secured the truss to the emerging building frame. An example of this procedure is found in the engraving of the construction of the Mormon Tabernacle in Salt Lake City, Utah.

Milliken Brothers devised a system eliminating the scaffolding method, wherein the trusses were assembled on the ground (usually in two or three sections) and then hoisted up by a system of four tall poles (called "gin poles"), pulleys and ropes and, finally, connected together in mid-air. At the Thirteenth Regiment Armory in Brooklyn, Milliken Brothers were able to erect three of the twelve 196 foot long trusses in five days.

The Iron-Work Contract

On November 29, 1893, the Articles of Agreement for the Iron-Work of the Auditorium were signed by Samuel Milliken, Jr., of Milliken Brothers Company, and E. H. Stokes, President, OGCMA. The steel frame work was to be finished and approved by the engineer, Lewis K. Davis, by March 15, 1894. The plans were marked as "Card No. 3137" in the company's records. A $50 per day penalty was agreed upon for every day after March 15 that the work was not completed.

The contract price was $15,500 stipulating payment of 80% on the monthly estimate of total value of contract work. Furthermore, Samuel Milliken, Sr., put the value of his house ($15,500) at 825 Central Avenue, South Plainfield, NJ, for a promissory bond note of $7,500, which was filed on December 8, 1893. While there is no documentation on why a bond note was signed, one reason may be the panic of 1893 that raised concerns about the general economic conditions of the time and the ability of contractors to meet their obligations.

The 11 pages of specifications filed on January 5, 1894, for the iron-work cover many topics, including the finish of the steel ("uniform in structure, free from cracks, flaws, blisters or buckles") with the "beam sides and edges smooth and full to gauge." Sample test bars were furnished for tests on tensile strength, limit of elasticity, elongation and ductility. The loads on trusses were to bear 40 lbs. per square foot, in addition to a roof bending stress of 30 lbs. per square foot for wind pressure. The factor of safety allowed was to be not less than four in all cases. The weight of the entire steel order was 550,000 pounds.

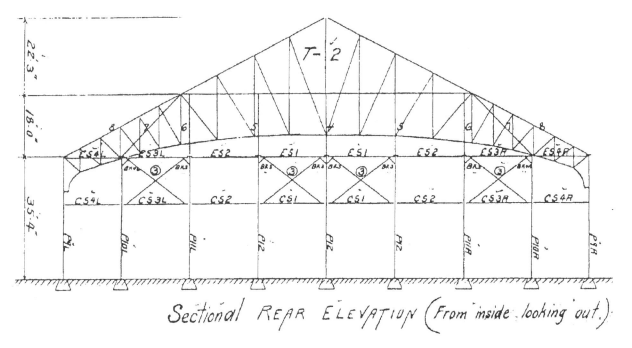

A Milliken Brothers' drawing showing a sectional view of the rear elevation with the rear wall, ceiling and truss work. The girders are sunk into concrete and granite footings under the floor.

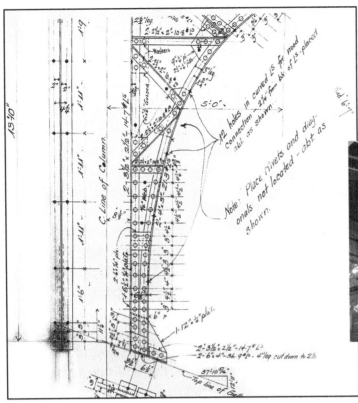

The details for fine workmanship included diameter of punch holes for rivets and bolts, threads on bolts, location of matching holes, facing and edges of plates "to be free from burrs or fins." All the steel was to be thoroughly cleaned from rust, scale, grease or other foreign materials and dried before being painted. All parts inaccessible for painting after being riveted up were painted beforehand in two coats. Other items in this contract, to list a few, included wind bracing, suspender slings, truss bolts, rigging, a cast or wrought iron coal slide cover (two feet in diameter with chain), hook and staple for boiler room coal chute and channel irons to act as guides to all doors next to the steel posts in the outside walls.

Ninety-two Days of Construction: Winter 1893-1894

The order was given on October 16 for the removal of the old Auditorium, which had a roof size of 19,856 square feet. A work crew of six to eight men labored diligently and without any injuries, salvaging items for use in other parts of the Camp Meeting grounds. Some timbers were used in the South End Pavilion, and the janitor's building was sold for a residence. Sale of old auditorium lumber netted $367.64. Iron settees, purchased from the Pitman Camp Meeting in 1874, were set aside in the park. On October 28, at 4:00 p.m., the last of the columns was pulled down before a small crowd of onlookers. It was a sad day, yet anticipation for the new and impressive facility mingled with fall air.

There is no official record of a surveyor or firm preparing the initial layout of the new building on the grounds. Clearly, someone performed survey services prior to the excavation for the foundation, because to make room for the larger building one row of tents on the north side of the Auditorium (Front Circle) was removed. Stokes reports that "every foot of the work (was) under the immediate inspection of B. F. Weed, Morristown, N.J., an expert surveyor." He was assisted by local Ocean Grove residents and Camp Meeting employees General John Patterson and Capt. Lewis Rainear.

Ground was broken for the foundation on December 2, 1893. Capt. Rainear, Superintendent of Ocean Grove, reports a total excavation of 173,934 square feet (or 6,442 cubic yards) of material, shoveled into carts and hauled off to fill in low areas around both Wesley and Fletcher Lake. The sand is classified as

February 21, 1894. The old auditorium is leveled and the foundation pit is dug. The four tall masts are in position to hoist the arches and truss work. On the left side is a four horse team pulling a carriage of iron beams.

Evesboro sand, a well-drained material with a depth to ground water between 10-15 feet. The excavation was probably accomplished by hand with the use of mule power pulling a scoop. An area of 161 feet by 225 feet was carefully sculpted into a gentle, sloping bowl, with a rough depth of eight feet at the platform/altar rail at the eastern end of the building. Deeper cellars were dug near the bases of the two smaller towers.

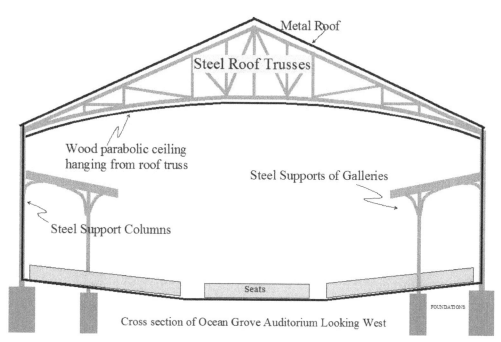

A cross section view of the Auditorium shows the foundational supports. The girders are set into concrete footings under the floor.

March 6, 1894. First iron truss in place. Several workers are standing on the truss.

March 12, 1894. Two main trusses are completed, and several angle trusses are in position.

Photo taken during the middle of construction, looking eastward through the framework. Note the two tall masts in the front and the concrete bases for the balcony (foreground). The Pavilion is visible on the lower left corner.

On Jan. 15, 1984, the Milliken Brothers sent the following note to Stokes, updating him on the progress of the work. Stokes immediately posted the letter in the *Ocean Grove Record*, and added, "I take great pleasure in laying this letter before the public, because the public ought to know just how things are moving. Before the time named in the letter, the carpenters will build their shops on the ground, and have commenced the work of preparing the lumber, so as to be ready for erecting (the Auditorium) as soon as the iron and steel work is up…Their contract is to have all their work finished by 20th day of June, 1894…I have always had and continue to feel the utmost confidence in our ultimate success…We expect to be ready to open the building for public worship on Sabbath, July 1, 1894."

Dr. E.H. Stokes, Ocean Grove, N.J.

DEAR SIR:

We beg to advise you in relation to the progress of the structural steel work at Ocean Grove Auditorium that we have delivered, and we understand they are set in place, the anchor bolts for the building. The advance bills of material to the rolling mills for rolling the material were sent some weeks ago and the material is all practically rolled. The exact bill of material for about one-half of the structure has been sent to the mills and the material is cut to finished lengths and shipped to the shops. The drawings for about two-thirds of the structure are finished and a large portion of this amount is now in the hands of the shops and the men are hard at work making the templets [sic] for punching and pushing the material as soon as it arrives. As soon as the templets are made and the material in the shops, the work of assembling and riveting up will commence and we hope in the course of three weeks to begin shipping the finished material. Of course, you understand that the above statement as regards the time of shipping the finished material is as near as we can judge at the present moment and depends largely on the railroad company and several other matters that are beyond our control. We are doing everything that is possible, however, to see that nothing prevents the rapid execution and delivery of this material. As you know, we have delivered the poles with which we erect this work and they are now at the site.

Trusting that the above will be of interest to you, we remain,

Very truly yours,
MILLIKEN BROS.

In February, the foundations for the steel work were poured. Workers dug 14 trenches: 6 feet by 7 feet wide and 9 feet in depth, filled with broken stone mixed with cement, to support the seven main truss arches. Each trench was finished with a cap-stone of granite, 2 feet 6 inches by 3 feet 6 inches, and one foot in thickness. All the granite capstones were contributed by George Potts, Esq., of Ocean Grove, from his own quarries in Pennsylvania, a donation of $1500 in raw stone materials. The quantity of broken stone under each main truss is about 15 tons, and the foundations and cap-stones have a crushing resistance of 29,000 pounds (14.5 tons) to the square inch. Foundations for the 18 gallery columns are also broken stone and cement laid in trenches 4 feet by 4 feet and 8 feet deep, about 8 tons of stone each.

Stokes was pleased to make a report to the public at this time: "I am quite well assured that no contractor for these foundations could have done the work better or cheaper than it has been. These foundations are all down and the capstones for the iron trusses will be in place in a week or ten days. The cellar walls are practically complete. That the weather should have remained so favorable for the work through the usually stormy months of December and January is matter for thanksgiving."

The Shore Press of Asbury Park reported pleasant weather for early March, as the Milliken Brothers workers lifted the first iron truss into position on Tuesday, March 6, 1894. L.K. Davis was Milliken's chief engineer of the steel and iron work. Foreman Wehmann explained how workmen assembled the iron trusses in two large sections on the ground, the larger section weighing 18 tons and the smaller section 8 tons, and then hoisted them up by a system of tall "gin" poles, pulleys and ropes. The sections were connected while suspended in midair, as workers clung to the iron frame, carefully riveting one section to the other. A good work team could heat, place and seal 225 rivets in one day.

March 19, 1894. Six of the seven main trusses are in position. The shape of the new Auditorium is emerging.

In Ocean Grove, the Milliken Brothers 30 member work crew completed the steel framing in 20 work days, with Sundays off, since the contract stipulated "Positively no work must be done on Sunday in Ocean Grove." After hoisting all of the seven expansive trusses into position, workers then crawled around the steel arches, attaching the 18 angle trusses for the balcony. By March 28, the frame for the new Auditorium was complete. The carpenters then began their work on the roof.

March 27, 1894. The mast poles are removed and the frames of the two smaller front towers are visible.

WAYNE T. BELL, JR. CINDY L. BELL DARRELL A. DUFRESNE

View from the attic showing the parabolic arch, catwalk, cross beams and roof truss attached to the arch.

Iron work supporting the gallery is visible on the lower level.

The tie rods – forming an "X" – add stabilization to the sections of the gallery.

Iron-Work Specifications

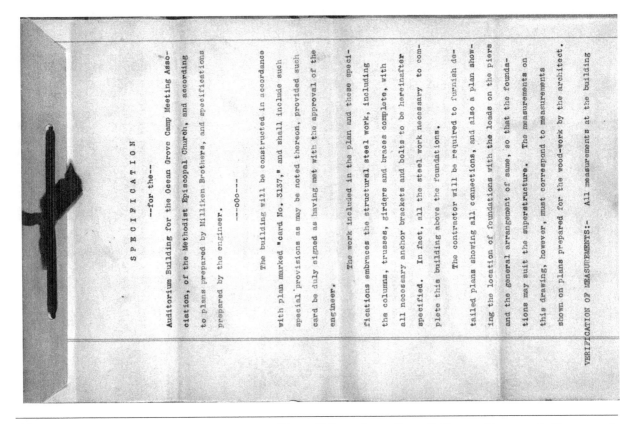

SPECIFICATION
--for the--

Auditorium Building for the Ocean Grove Camp Meeting Association, of the Methodist Episcopal Church, and according to plans prepared by Milliken Brothers, and specifications prepared by the engineer.

----oOo----

The building will be constructed in accordance with plan marked "card No. 3137," and shall include such special provisions as may be noted thereon, provided such card be duly signed as having met with the approval of the engineer.

The work included in the plan and these specifications embraces the structural steel work, including the columns, trusses, girders and braces complete, with all necessary anchor brackets and bolts to be hereinafter specified. In fact, all the steel work necessary to complete this building above the foundations.

The contractor will be required to furnish detailed plans showing all connections, and also a plan showing the location of foundations with the loads on the piers and the general arrangement of same, so that the foundations may suit the superstructure. The measurements on this drawing, however, must correspond to measurements shown on plans prepared for the wood-work by the architect.

VERIFICATION OF MEASUREMENTS:- All measurements at the building

-2-

will be verified by the engineer and the contractor notified, so that the work may be proceeded with with all possible expedition.

TIME FOR ORDERING WORK:- Work not to be ordered until all plans are approved and a set returned signed by the engineer in charge.

SPECIFICATION OF QUALITY.

GENERAL:- All material used shall be of steel in accordance with the following specification, except that the contractor shall have the right to substitute for brackets, fittings, rivets or unimportant members, iron of first-class quality. All important members carrying strains must be furnished in steel.

FINISH:- All steel must be uniform in structure, free from cracks, flaws, blisters or buckles. The sides and edges must be smooth and full to gauge. Shapes which are fuller on one side than on another will not be accepted. No special process or provision of manufacture will be demanded as long as the quality fulfills the requirements of this specification.

STANDARD TEST PIECES:- From each heat of steel sample test bars shall be furnished of finished size one inch square, and of clear length of minimum section 8 inches long with curved ends where it meets the part placed in the jaws of the testing machine. From these standard test bars the ultimate tensile strength, limit of elasticity, elongation and

-3-

ductility shall be determined.

ULTIMATE TENSILE STRENGTH:- The ultimate tensile strength shall not be less than 60,000 lbs. or more than 68,000 lbs. per square inch.

ELASTIC LIMIT:- The elastic limit shall not be less than 32,000 pounds per square inch.

ELONGATION:- Elongation shall not be less than 20 per cent. in eight inches.

BENDING:- All steel must bend cold to 180 degrees without sign of fracture to a curve, the inner radius of which equals the thickness of the piece tested.

RIVETS:- All rivets shall be of iron and must be double refined and must bend cold until the sides are in close contact without sign of fracture on the convex side of curve.

NUMBER OF PIECES TESTED:- At least one test piece for breaking and one test piece for bending will be furnished by the manufacturer, free of cost, for each order of iron. One test piece of each kind will be furnished by the manufacturer, free of cost, for every cast of steel. In case the owner or engineer in charge desires extra test pieces, these will be furnished and tested at $5.00 each extra.

WORKMANSHIP.

PUNCHING:- In punching iron or steel the die shall not ex-

concentric to the shank and fit tightly to the base of the head. No loose or imperfect rivets will be allowed.

PIN HOLES:- All pin holes must be accurately drilled to right angles to the axis of the member, unless otherwise specified. Any pieces not adjustable, the variation center to center of holes must not exceed 1-32nd of an inch, unless specified. The diameter of pin hole must not exceed the diameter of the pin by more than 1-32nd of an inch. All members must be perfectly straight before drilling.

EYE BARS, LOOP ENDS, CLEVICES, ETC.:- The exact detail of the heads of eye bars, ends of loop eyes, clevices, turn buckles, etc., will be left to the manufacturer to suit his standards, providing that first, the details do not interfere with any of the work, and second, that the parts are stronger than the body of bar as may be determined by tests of full size members. In the case of eye bars no welds will be allowed in the body of bar. Pairs of clevices must have right and left hand thread; turn buckles must be open; no sleeve nuts will be allowed.

UPSET ENDS OF BARS:- All bars in tension which have a thread cut in them must be upset on ends so that the diameter of the bar at the base of thread will be at least 1-16" larger than the diameter of the bar before upsetting.

FACING:- All compression members which bear on other members and which are not full splice but depend on abut-

ceed the diameter of punch by more than 1-16th of an inch. All holes shall be clean and smooth.

ACCURACY OF RIVET HOLES:- Rivet holes must be so accurately made that when the parts are assembled a hot rivet 1-16th of an inch diameter less than the hole, will enter without straining the member by drift pins. Holes for rivets must not be made more than 1-16" diameter greater than the diameter of the cold rivet intended to connect the work.

REAMING:- Rivet holes in the iron will not be required to be reamed, but preference will be given to work which is punched 1-16" smaller than the required finished diameter and then reamed to full size.

SPLICE PLATES AND CONNECTIONS:- Great care must be used in spacing rivet holes for splices or connecting plates, to see that the holes are directly opposite.

BOLTS IN SHEARING:- Bolts connecting pieces which are subject to shearing and which are over 3-4" in diameter must be "skinned." The holes must be reamed so that the bolts go in with a driving fit.

THREADS ON BOLTS, PINS, ETC.:- All screw threads must be of the U. S. standard V-shaped thread.

RIVETING:- All rivets must be machine driven wherever practicable; the rivet shall be held by the machine until the head is perfectly formed. The rivet must be upset to completely fill the hole. The head must be full size and

-6-

ting surfaces, must be planed or faced in a machine.

FINISH OF PLATES:- All plates and bars under 30" wide must be rolled in grooved rolls or universal mill, except for webs of built up members, webs of riveted girders, gusset connecting plates and bed plates. Sheared plates must be cut straight and the edges must be free from burrs or fins.

FINISH OF PIECES:- All members must be straight, and unless otherwise specified, free from twists, winds or buckles and all parts of a compound piece must be free from any open joints.

SUPPORTING MEMBERS:- All stiffeners, supporting plates and brackets must have a full bearing after being riveted up.

FACE OF COLUMNS:- All columns which require to be faced on the ends must have the ends planed and the planed surfaces must be faced at right angles to the axis of column.

INSPECTION AND ACCEPTANCE OF MATERIAL.

OF MATERIAL AT MILLS:- The owner or engineer in charge will either inspect, or appoint a representative to inspect, at his own expense, the material at the rolling mill during process of manufacture. The contractor must see that the mill furnishes, without cost to the owner, the necessary test pieces as provided for in these specifications and also a testing machine and necessary apparatus for making the tests and to give said inspector free access to the works and all necessary facilities for making these tests. The expense of the inspector will be borne by the owner. The

-7-

owner reserves the right to do away with the above form of inspection, in which case the mill must make the tests and forward the broken test pieces to the owner with an affidavit stating that the test pieces so furnished were a part of the lot of iron or steel from which the work for this structure was rolled. This affidavit must be made by an officer in authority connected with the rolling mill and who knew the facts stated in the affidavit. The contractor and mill in this latter case will only be responsible for surface finish and defects in the work.

OF MATERIAL AT SHOPS:- The owner or engineer in charge will either inspect, or appoint a representative to inspect, the work while being assembled in the shop. Free access to the shops must be given the inspector. The owner will pay all expenses of said inspector. In case the owner desires to do away with this inspection the contractor will still be held responsible for the finish of the work.

VARIATION IN WEIGHT:- A variation in weight of more than 2 1/2 per cent. either more or less than the weight called for on the drawings may be cause for rejection.

NOTIFICATION TO INSPECTOR:- The contractor must notify the inspector long enough in advance of rolling and work at the shop, to enable him to be on hand. If, after such notice the inspector be not present, then the mill is to proceed with the tests and keep a report.

TIME TO START ERECTION:- In case the metal work rests on brick

pine are hung from each truss. The slings for same are to be of band iron 2" x 3/8", suspended by 1" rods and 8 ft. apart. The junction between these 8" x 12" girders and steel columns, is to be 6" x 12" angle brackets with two 1" bolts.

The above extra work must be to the satisfaction of the architect.

WIND BRACING:- All wind bracing must be done in accordance with plans to be furnished by iron contractor and subject to the approval of the engineer.

Contractor for iron work must furnish all necessary ties, straps, bridle irons, brackets, bolts, etc., that may be required by the carpenter in the construction of the building, as shown by drawings prepared by the architect. He shall also furnish suspender slings at front square corner hips and under 8" x 10" beams, in angle panels, front and rear. Also one cast or wrought iron coal slide cover, 2 ft. in diameter, with chain, hook and staple for boiler room coal chute.

All wooden truss bolts of the following size: 4' long; 1" in diameter and 2' long; 3/4" in diameter, for small trusses in gallery front. Shall furnish and set 2 inch channel irons to act as guides to all doors next to steel posts in outside walls, about 20 feet long with proper holes for rope and pulley to work in, and bolt the pulleys for same, which will be furnished by carpenter, securely to channels.

or stone work, the engineer in charge cannot order the contractor to set his work until the entire tier on floor is leveled off complete, except in such cases where the contractor will have six working days for a full gang of men without changing his rigging to an entirely different part of the building.

PAINTING:- All work must be thoroughly cleaned from rust, scale, grease or other foreign materials, and dried before being painted, after which it must be painted with one coat of National Lead Company's red lead, mixed with pure linseed oil in the following parts, to wit: 5 lbs. of oil to 18 lbs. of red lead.

All parts inaccessible for painting, after being riveted up, must be painted two coats before. All parts which have machine service, or which are bored or threaded, must be coated with white lead and tallow before shipment.

No painting will be allowed during wet weather.

Parts on which the paint has been damaged during the course of erection, must be repainted to the satisfaction of the engineer without extra expense to owner.

EXTRA WORK INCLUDED IN CONTRACT:- Contractor for iron work must furnish all necessary lugs to support purlins, riveted on side of trusses for the side and bottom of wooden purlins, and have two bolt holes and 3/4" bolts for same. These purlins are to be set vertically and not perpendicularly to the rake of rafter and 8 ft. apart.

Transverse wooden girders of 8" x 12" Georgia

than four in all cases.

NOTE:- Where the word "owner" or "engineer in charge" appears in this specification, it is intended to mean The Ocean Grove Camp Meeting Association of the Methodist Episcopal Church, and its engineer, Mr. Lewis K. Davis, appointed by said Association, and where the word "contractor" is mentioned in this specification it is understood to mean Milliken Brothers. Positively no work must be done on Sunday at Ocean Grove.

ERECTION.

GENERAL:- All work must be erected and connected complete according to the plans. All columns must be plumb and true and all floors must be level unless specially specified. All trusses must be straight, true and out of wind. The use of shims or wedges will not be allowed. All pieces must come to a proper bearing without being distorted or strained. All bolts and rods must be made tight. All pins over 2" diameter must be put in place with a pilot nut.

RIVETING:- Rivets must be carefully driven while hot and must completely fill the holes and have full, tight heads. All holes must be exactly opposite or they must be reamed.

RIGGING:- The contractor must furnish all necessary tools and power to properly erect and complete the work. The tools and rigging must be so constructed as not to interfere with the other contractors. The owners will furnish all necessary permits or permissions to attach guys or locate tools or material on any public or private property not owned by the owners of this building, but contractor must be responsible for all damage caused to such property.

LOADS:- Loads on trusses to be figured as follows:
Roof trusses will bear 40 lbs. per square foot, in addition to bending stress of 30 lbs. per square foot for wind pressure. Factor of safety allowed, not less

-2-

the time aforesaid, in a good, workman-like and substantial manner, to the satisfaction and under the direction of the said engineer or his assistant; to be testified under the hand of the said engineer by a writing or certificate, and shall and will provide good, proper and sufficient material of all kinds whatsoever, of the best kind of material of the character required by the specifications as shall be proper and sufficient for the completion and finishing of all the works of said building mentioned in the said specifications and drawings, for the sum of fifteen thousand five hundred dollars ($15,500), and will accept payment of said sum in the amounts, at the times and upon the conditions hereinafter mentioned.

SECOND:- And the said parties of the first part do hereby, for themselves, their heirs, executors and administrators, covenant, promise and agree to and with the said parties of the second part, their heirs, executors and administrators, that they, the said parties of the first part, shall and will, in consideration of the covenants and agreements of the parties of the second part being strictly performed and kept by the said parties of the second part, and upon the conditions in this agreement contained, well and truly pay, or cause to be paid, unto the said parties of the second part, their executors, administrators or assigns, the sum of fifteen thousand five hundred dollars ($15,500), lawful money of the United States of America, in manner following, that is to say:

80% on monthly estimate of total value of work

ARTICLES OF AGREEMENT, for Iron-Work of Auditorium at Ocean Grove, New Jersey, made this 28th day of November, 1893, in triplicate, between the OCEAN GROVE CAMP MEETING ASSOCIATION, of the Methodist Episcopal Church, parties of the first part, and MILLIKEN BROTHERS, of New York City, parties of the second part,

WITNESSETH:

The parties hereto, for and in consideration of the premises, and one dollar by each to the other in hand paid, the receipt whereof is hereby acknowledged, and of the covenants and agreements herein contained, agree for themselves and their respective heirs, executors and administrators, as follows:

FIRST:- The said parties of the second part do hereby, for themselves, their heirs, executors and administrators, covenant, promise and agree to and with the said parties of the first part, or their assigns, that they, the said parties of the second part, their executors or administrators shall and will, for the consideration herein named, on or before the 15th day of March, 1894, well and sufficiently erect and finish all iron-work in strict accordance with the specifications. Drawings to be made by said Milliken Bros. in accordance with said specifications, subject to the examination and approval of the engineer in charge, and duly signed by the parties hereto, and annexed and made a part of this agreement, marked by such number or letter as may hereinafter be decided, within

able to pay in discharging any lien on the said premises or claim made obligatory in consequence of the default of the parties of the second part.

FOURTH:- It is mutually agreed that the parties of the second part, as general and independent contractors, shall assume, and they hereby agree to assume, all risks and all liability for injury or damage to persons or property, of every description, connected with or arising out of the construction of said building, whether relating to the building itself or said works or materials or other things used and employed in completing said works, or to any other person or persons who may have any cause of action whatsoever by reason of any matter arising during or connected with the construction of said building, and including any claim of the owners of properties adjoining the lands upon which said building is to be erected, against all of which injuries and damage to persons and property the parties of the second part, having control over said work, must properly guard, and must make good all damage from whatever cause, they hereby indemnifying the parties of the first part from and against any and all liability, loss or damage resulting from or connected with any such injury or damage.

FIFTH:- The parties of the second part, for the considerations aforesaid, further agree that time is of the essence of this contract, and that if the said building shall not be fully completed on the 15th day of March, 1894, in accordance with the terms of this con-

done upon the ground, balance due after thirty days from completion and acceptance of work, provided that in each of said cases a certificate shall be obtained, signed by the said engineer, that the amount to be paid is equal to 80% of the work done and that the work upon such building has, up to that time, been in accordance with the plans and specifications, and satisfactory to him and that no mechanics' liens have been filed for labor done or material supplied for the said iron-work of the building, and that he is satisfied that there are no claims outstanding upon which any such liens can be based, and the parties of the second part shall supply the said engineer with evidence satisfactory to the said engineer for the purposes of said certificate.

THIRD:- For the consideration aforesaid the parties of the second part further covenant and agree that, if at any time there shall be any lien or claim for which, if established, the said parties of the first part might be made liable and which would be chargeable to the said parties of the second part, the parties of the first part shall have the right to retain out of any payments then due, or thereafter to become due, an amount sufficient to completely indemnify the parties of the first part against such lien or claim until the same shall be effectually satisfied, discharged and cancelled, and should there prove to be any such lien or claim after all payments are made, the parties of the second part shall refund to the parties of the first part, all the money which the parties of the first part shall be legally li-

or to become due to the parties of the second part under this agreement. And if the said engineer shall certify that such refusal, neglect or failure is sufficient ground for such action, (which certificate shall be final and conclusive upon the parties hereto,) the parties of the first part shall also be at liberty to terminate the employment of the parties of the second part for the said work and to enter upon the premises and take possession of all materials, tools and implements thereon, and to employ any other person or persons to finish the work and to provide the materials therefor, and in case of such discontinuance of the employment of the parties of the second part, they shall not be entitled to receive any further payment under this contract until the said work shall be wholly finished, at which time, if the unpaid balance of the amount to be paid under this agreement shall exceed the expense incurred by the parties of the first part in finishing said work, together with the sum of fifty dollars ($50) per day for each day's delay in the completion of said works after the said 15th day of March, 1894, which shall result from such refusal, neglect or failure of the parties of the second part (which sum of fifty dollars ($50) per day is hereby agreed upon as liquidated damages to the parties of the first part for such delay,) and together with any other damage resulting to the parties of the first part from such refusal, neglect or failure of the parties of the second part, such

tract that they, the said parties of the second part, will pay to the parties of the first part the sum of fifty dollars ($50) for each and every working day after said 15th day of March, 1894, until said building shall be finally completed. Said sum of fifty dollars ($50) per day being hereby agreed upon as liquidated damages, to be retained by the parties of the first part and deducted from the balance, which would otherwise be owing to the parties of the second part upon the completion of the building in accordance with this contract.

SIXTH:- It is further mutually agreed that should the parties of the second part at any time refuse or neglect to supply a sufficiency of proper, skilled workmen, or of materials of the proper quality, or fail in any respect to prosecute the work with diligence, or fail in the performance of any of the agreements on their part herein contained, such refusal, neglect or failure being certified by the said engineer (and whose certificate as to such refusal, neglect or failure shall be final and conclusive upon the parties hereto) or if the parties of the second part shall become insolvent or otherwise unable themselves to perform the works as specified and conditioned in this agreement, then, in either or any of said events, the parties of the first part shall be at liberty, after three days' written notice to the parties of the second part, to provide any such materials or labor, or both, and to deduct the cost from any money then due

excess shall be paid by the parties of the first part to the parties of the second part, but if such expense, together with said liquidated and other damages shall exceed such unpaid balance, the parties of the second part shall pay the amount of such excess to the parties of the first part. The expense so incurred by the parties of the first part, together with the liquidated and other damages herein provided for, shall be audited and certified by the said engineer, whose certificate thereof shall be conclusive upon the parties hereto.

SEVENTH:- The parties of the second part, at their own proper cost and charges, are to provide all manner of materials and labor, scaffolding, implements, moulds, models and cartage of every description, for the due performance of the several erections, or incident thereto.

EIGHTH:- Should the parties of the first part at any time during the progress of the said works request any alteration, deviation, addition or omission from this contract, they shall be at liberty to do so, and the same shall in no way affect or make void the contract, but may be added to or deducted from the amount of the contract, as the case may be, by a fair and reasonable valuation.

NINTH:- The parties of the second part shall make no claim for additional work, unless the same shall

be done in pursuance of a written order or orders from the engineer approved by the owners, and notice of all such claims shall be made to the engineer in writing within ten days after the beginning of such work.

TENTH:- Should any dispute arise respecting the true construction or meaning of the drawings or specifications, the same shall be decided by the engineer, and his decision shall be final and conclusive. But should any dispute arise respecting the true value of the extra work, or of the works omitted, the same shall be valued by competent arbitrators, one to be appointed by the parties of the first part, and the other by the parties of the second part, and these two shall choose a third, and a decision of any two of these three arbitrators shall be binding upon both parties.

ELEVENTH:- It is further mutually agreed that the specifications and drawings are intended to co-operate, so that any works exhibited in the drawings and not mentioned in the specifications, or vice versa, are to be executed the same as if they were mentioned in the specifications and set forth in the drawings, to the true meaning and intention of the said drawings and specifications, without any extra charge whatsoever. And should it appear that the work hereby intended to be done, or any of the matters relative thereto, are not sufficiently detailed or explained in the said drawings or in the said specifications, the parties of the second part shall apply to the engineer for such further drawings or explanations as may be necessary, and shall conform to the same as part of this contract, so far as the same shall be consistent with the said drawings and specifications, without any extra charge whatsoever therefor.

TWELFTH:- The parties of the second part will insure the works to cover their interest in the same, from time to time as required, and for any loss of the parties of the second part by fire or any other cause, the parties of the first part will not under any circumstances be answerable or accountable; but the Parties of the first part may protect said works at their option, by insurance to cover the interest when payments shall have been made to the parties of the second part; it being understood that the meaning of this clause is that the interest of the parties of the first part in said works begins when and as payments shall have been made to said parties of the second part, and that if such last named portion of the works shall be injured or destroyed by fire, the parties of the first part shall bear and pay the resulting loss.

THIRTEENTH:- The parties of the second part shall give their personal attention to the execution of the works, and the building and its immediate surroundings shall be cleaned of all rubbish and surplus materials and left in a clean, orderly and trim condition at the close of the works.

FOURTEENTH:- The parties of the second part further agree that the engineer and the parties of the first part may visit the works in person, or by deputy, as often as they shall deem necessary. The parties of the second part shall provide safe and adequate means for the inspection of the works by the engineer and by the parties of the first part, or the appointee of either, and shall furnish the engineer incidental help which the engineer may need for examining and measuring the works. The labor, materials and workmanship, including methods of work and the order in which the works are to be performed, shall be under the supervision of the engineer, and subject to his approval or rejection. Any material and work, or method of work, disapproved by the engineer, shall be replaced, or changed, by the parties of the second part upon the engineer's requirement and to the engineer's satisfaction.

The parties of the second part shall, within twenty-four hours after receiving written notice from the engineer to that effect, proceed to remove from the grounds or building all material condemned by him, whether worked or unworked, and take down all portions of the work which the engineer shall condemn as unsound or improper or as in any way failing to conform to the drawings and specifications and to the conditions of this contract. The parties of the second part shall cover, protect and exercise due diligence to secure the work from injury, and all damage happening to the same by their neglect shall be made good by them.

The parties of the second part shall discharge any foreman or other employee who shall, in the judgment of the engineer, be unfaithful, unskillful or remiss in the performance of his work, or guilty of riotous, disrespectful or otherwise improper conduct, and no person so dismissed shall be employed again on the works without the written consent of the engineer.

FIFTEENTH:- The supervision of the materials and works by the engineer shall not relieve the parties of the second part from liability to make good any defects of material, construction or workmanship which may be discovered after the engineer's approval of the works, in part or as a whole. The parties of the second part shall, without any compensation beyond the money consideration upon which this agreement is based, make good any imperfections, defects, or structural failures which may be discovered or which may occur, within one year from the day of the completion of the works in general.

It is further mutually agreed between the parties that no certificate given or payment made under this contract, except the final certificate and final payment, shall be conclusive evidence of the performance or this contract, either wholly or in part, against any claim of the parties of the first part, and no payment shall be construed to be an acceptance of any defective work.

SIXTEENTH:- It is further understood and agreed that said Milliken Brothers having made the estimated weight of the entire steel work, and having duly stated and acknowledged same to be 515,000 lbs., should the finished structure not weigh the above amount, namely, 515,000 lbs., a reduction on total cost will be made for every pound thereunder. An allowance will be made, however, of 2 1/2¢ for variations either above or below said 515,000 lbs., for which no charge will be made. Should the finished weight exceed the said amount of 515,000 lbs., no extra charge will be allowed.

SEVENTEENTH:- The parties of the first part shall obtain any legal permits necessary, but the parties of the second part shall comply with any and all local laws, ordinances and regulations which control or limit, in any sense, the actions of those engaged upon the works, or affect the materials or the transportation or disposition of them.

IN WITNESS WHEREOF, We have hereunto set our hands and seals this 29th day of November, 1893.

Signed, sealed and delivered

in the presence of

STATE OF NEW JERSEY, }
COUNTY OF Union } ss.:
COUNTY OF ~~MONMOUTH~~

Samuel Milliken Jr., being duly sworn, deposes and says: That he resides at No. 531 Central av in the City of Plainfield N.J., and that the value of his property over and above all debts and liabilities incurred by him is over Fifteen Thousand Dollars ($15,000.00); that he is fully responsible for the amount of his obligations on the foregoing bond by him executed.

Sworn and subscribed this 8th day of December 1893.

[signatures]
Notary Public N.J.

STATE OF NEW JERSEY, }
COUNTY OF MONMOUTH. } ss.:

..............., being duly sworn, deposes and says: That he resides at No. .... in the City of ...., and that the value of his property over and above all debts and liabilities incurred by him is over ($); that he is fully responsible for the amount of his obligations on the foregoing bond by him executed.

Sworn and subscribed this }
.... day of ...., 1893. }

KNOW ALL MEN BY THESE PRESENTS: That we, Milliken Bros of New York City and Saml Milliken Jr of Plainfield N.J.

are held and firmly bound unto the Ocean Grove Camp Meeting Association, of the Methodist Episcopal Church, in the full and just sum of seven thousand seven hundred and fifty ($7,750) dollars, lawful money of the United States, to be paid to the said Ocean Grove Camp Meeting Association, or the Methodist Episcopal Church, or to its proper agent or attorney duly authorized to receive the same as liquidated damages; to which payment, well and truly to be made and done, we bind our and every of us, our and every of our heirs, executors and administrators, in the whole and for the whole, jointly and severally, firmly by these presents.

Sealed with our seal and dated this 8th day of December , 1893.

The condition of the above obligation is such that, if Milliken Brothers, their heirs, executors and administrators, do and shall well and truly execute the contract hereto annexed, which they have entered into with the said Ocean Grove Camp Meeting Association, of the Methodist Episcopal Church, by which said Milliken Brothers, conforming in all respects to said contract, same being hereto annexed; the foregoing obligation to be void and of none effect, otherwise to remain in full force and virtue in law.

Signed, sealed and delivered
in the presence of
[signatures]

3366

Contract

The Ocean Grove Camp
Meeting Association of
the M. E. Church
and
Milliken Brothers

Filed January 5. 1894
Theo Aumack

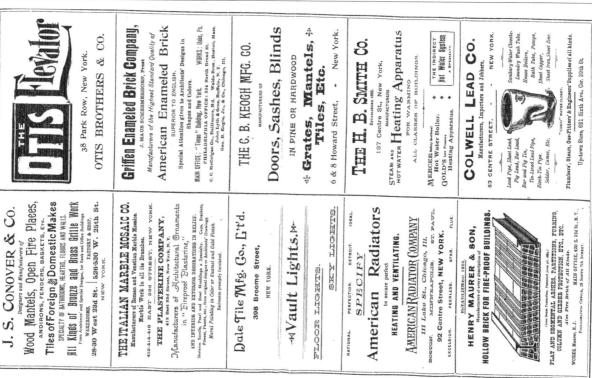

THE NEW AUDITORIUM—Erected 1894.

In this photo from the 1894 Annual Report of the OGCMA, there is no staircase on the southeast side. The outline of the two small towers frame the colored-glass windows. There are two chimneys on the front and two massive cast iron urns along Pilgrim Pathway.

AUDITORIUM, OCEAN GROVE, N. J.

Careful examination of this advertisement by Hopkins & Roberts has tantalizing clues to Camp's original design. Note the covered stairways to the gallery on the front southeast corner and rear southwest side. Visible in this sketch on the southeast corner is Camp's aborted idea for the ground floor doors to slide apart and overhead.

Chapter Five

CARPENTRY SPECIFICATIONS

The carpentry and sheet metal roofing contract was awarded to Hopkins and Roberts of 245 Broadway in New York. The firm specialized in the building of churches and interior renovations, including major houses of worship in New York (e.g., Marble Collegiate Church at 7th Street and Second Avenue) and other sites upstate and on Long Island. An advertisement by Hopkins and Roberts in George Kramer's 1897 *The What, How and Why of Church Building* is one source of an early sketch of the 1894 Auditorium.

The contract was signed by company owners LeRoy Hopkins and John B. Roberts on January 13, 1894, at an agreement price of $26,000. A bond of $12,000 was required by the Camp Meeting Association. The work was to be completed on or before June 20, 1894. Given this large sum of money – it is the single largest contract, costing $10,000 more than the iron work - the contract stipulated the following payment schedule:

- First payment of $4,250: when all the timber of the sides, roof, floors and galleries are in place.
- Second payment of $7,000: when metal roof is on, side walls enclosed where permanent and parabolic ceiling (is) in place.
- Third payment of $6,750: completion of cupolas, floors, gutters and leaders installed, platform and altar built, and office part studded and furred, ready for plastering.
- Fourth payment of $4,500: when sash is in, doors hung, galleries finished, outside stairs and porches done.
- Fifth payment of $3,500: when the building is complete and after the expiration of 15 days, and when all Drawings and Specifications have been returned to Frederick T. Camp, Architect.

The contract is very specific regarding the quality of timber: "square sawn, sound and free from defects, sap or shakes and well-seasoned." Most of the timber was North Carolina yellow pine, except for specific items. Other woods included Pennsylvania white hemlock, white pine, oak, spruce and American chestnut.

The iron skeleton of the new Auditorium was complete by March 28, and the Milliken Brothers removed their tall mast

This 2010 view of the south façade showing the exit stairway, three tiers of door panels, roof towers and dormer, demonstrate the simplicity and symmetry of the exterior design.

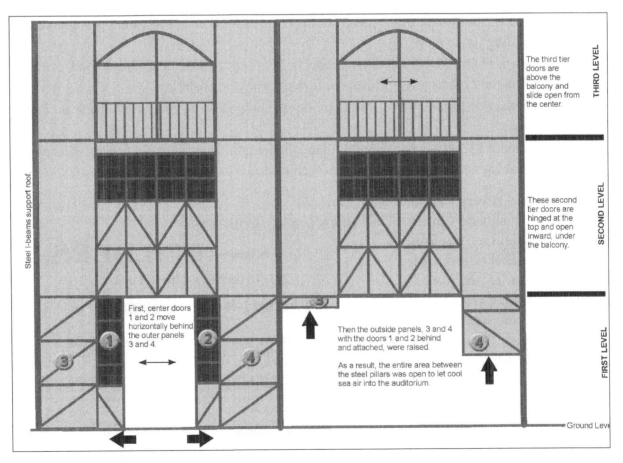

Schematic of the process of how the four panel doors were to be raised overhead.

The third tier doors are above the balcony and slide open from the center.

These second tier doors are hinged at the top and open inward, under the balcony.

First, center doors 1 and 2 move horizontally behind the outer panels 3 and 4.

Then the outside panels, 3 and 4 with the doors 1 and 2 behind and attached, were raised.

As a result, the entire area between the steel pillars was open to let cool sea air into the auditorium.

THIRD LEVEL

SECOND LEVEL

FIRST LEVEL

Steel I-beams support roof.

Ground Level

poles from the site. The carpenters followed with preparations for the corrugated and galvanized roof. Floor beams were first placed all around the interior on the iron and steel supports of the gallery. The eastern front of the building took shape, with its semi-circle of offices and waiting rooms and two cupolas. Larger and more imposing turrets rose from the apex of the roof at both ends. The Bishop Janes Tabernacle, a smaller building on the south side of the Auditorium, was turned into a woodworking shop for door assembly, railings, moldings, etc.

With less than three months to complete the carpentry, the Hopkins & Roberts work team met with several challenges, as reported in the *Shore Press*. A furious storm the second week of April closed down operations for several days, but "all hands were out early, and the banging commenced anew" after the weather passed. By April 28, the roof was on, and workmen began the tedious process of riveting the corrugated galvanized iron roofing sheets. As the small towers neared completion, The *Shore Press* reported that "the building (had) a kind of oriental magnificence which will be appreciated by all who have an eye for the graceful in architectural designs."

Sliding Doors

Some congregants expressed concern in the local paper that "Oh my, the new Auditorium is all shut up like a regular meeting house." Having that open-air feeling was deep-seated for Ocean Grove camp meeting worshippers. There were to be 266 openings, with "all the lower story thrown as completely open as the old one," and the ground level doors could be closed if the wind was too strong.

One can still see the 1 inch by 5 inch recessed area that provided a hand hold to lift the door panel.

The paneled doors on the main floor are of (solid select) "sound white pine, with very few knots allowed." The original plan for opening up all sliding doors on the ground level was complicated: four doors, each measuring 8 feet by 13 feet were hung in a four-panel format between two steel support columns. The two center doors with glass panes were to slide apart and behind the adjacent solid panels; then, the two sets of doors were lifted up to the second tier, thus opening all four spaces. An iron counter weight on a chain boxed in a vertical channel next to

  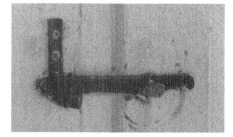

The simple door latch consists of two parts: an iron 2 ½ inch hanging bar (above) and a 7 inch hooked-shaped bar. The hook bar swivels down to latch behind the lag bolt; the hanging bar secures it in position. The hanging bar prevents the hook bar from being raised by a thin blade from the outside.

the steel columns gave a struggling usher the ability to lift the heavy doors.

This sliding door arrangement for the first tier was eventually abandoned, probably due to the heavy weight of the combined doors and jamming of the iron tracks. Now only the two glass pane doors are pushed open on a single overhead track. Many of the iron weights and chains are still hanging in the boxed channels. Also, if you look carefully at the bottom of the present sliding doors, you will see a one inch by five inch hollow area. This recessed space permitted an Auditorium Usher to grip and lift the door to the overhead position. Still found on the doors are the original wrought-iron barn door locks. The language of the contract is very specific regarding the arrangement of the doors on the second and third tier: "The second or middle range (doors) will be hinged with the strongest strap hinges each, and

The second tier panels are opened inward by a series of ropes and pulleys.

will swing up open, to soffit of gallery. They will be opened and shut by proper ropes and pulleys and other hardware selected by the Architect." Additionally, "the sliding doors on the upper gallery level (will) slide and roll to the sides on five foot sheaves and iron tracts." This arrangement of upper level doors is still in use today.

On opening day at the Auditorium in 1894, every main floor door was safely stored overhead, as people flowed through the many open doorways. Essentially, Camp's door design created the desired effect of a true outdoor camp meeting assembly, allowing maximum air circulation and shielding the worshipers from rain or sun. Now, in 2012, only half the doors in each panel open, decreasing ventilation.

Up above the ceiling, a catwalk parallels the steel arch. The wooden chamber (upper right corner) housed parts of an early organ.

Flooring

As congregants passed through the open doors, they stepped on to a good, solid floor. The previous Auditoriums had straw in the aisles, so a hard floor would bring "relief from anxieties about fire from careless lighting of matches or smoking of segars." Laying of the floor began after the ceiling. Interestingly enough, the original design specification lists "asphalt cement on sand" for the floor. But there was a change in the plans, as the lower flooring is southern hard pine boards running across 2 inch by 4 inch by 12 foot beams supported on brick columns. Fifteen hundred yards of "cocoa matting" was used to cover the platform, inside of the altar, aisles and stairways. This was considered "first class and heavy quality," and would reduce the sound of those walking in and out. Mill shavings were used as a sound reduction method in the balcony.

Hanging Curtain in the Rear

There is one specification which apparently was not completed, as it is not observable in early photos of the interior: a curtain under the rear gallery at the west end. This was to be made "in folding style out of 5/8 double surfaced North Carolina pine ceiling on 5/8 frames, tails and braces as detailed," and to "be arranged to fold on hinges by pulleys and ropes in manner as detailed and directed by the architect." Perhaps this curtain was for acoustical purposes.

The odd-sized pieces of lumber nailed on the ceiling helps keep the wainscot boards flush. The straight pipe in the middle is part of the air pressure/fire suppression system for the building.

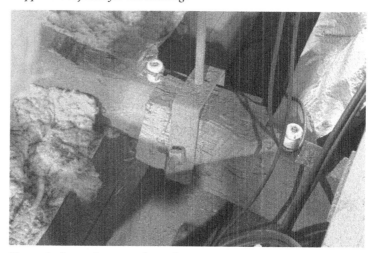

The end of a 21 foot cross beam between two arches. This beam in turn rests on the arch and is held in place by a U-shaped steel saddle bolted to the steel rod. This is truly a "hanging ceiling." Note the remains of the old porcelain knob and tube wiring.

Speaker's Platform

The speaker's platform at the east end was constructed of "1⅛ inch by 3 inch North Carolina pine, tongue and groove and blind nailed butts, perfectly joined and braided and smoothed off immediately after laying." Platform girders 8 inch by 10 inch of hemlock supported the platform beams of 3 inch by 12 inch on 24 inch centers. Also installed on the platform was a square section (13 feet by 13 feet) of old boards from the previous auditorium platform. (It is interesting to note that in 1974, a similar activity occurred when a floor section from the Grand Ole Opry Show at the old Ryman Auditorium in Nashville, Tennessee, was removed and reinstalled in the new Opryland, USA, complex.)

Interior view of the complex frame construction of the third tier door openings.

At the rear of the speaker's platform, a sounding board was constructed of the same materials as the ceiling and the curves, "secured to 2 inch by 4 inch studding furring on 16 inch centers, braced to main walls and finished with a neat wooden cornice, cresting out of 1½ inch white pine cut in pattern shown or detailed."

The sounding board placed over the speaker's platform was "constructed of dry seasoned spruce in wedge shaped pieces, ⅞ inch by 3 inch, tongue and groove, matched and dressed two sides, blind nailed onto curved furring and suspended by wire rope from ceiling timbers." Further details specify the curve of the sounding board: "it will be about 25 feet wide at top, 15 feet wide at bottom and about 25 feet in length."

Hanging Ceiling

The hanging wainscot ceiling, referred to in the contract as "Ceiling Sounding Board," was reported by carpenters working on the building to be the most difficult work of the project. It is made "of ⅝ inch by 4 inch dressed and matched well-seasoned North Carolina pine, tongue and groove, beaded and free from any larger than pin knots, blind nailed to ceiling timbers and furring, and butts well made and beaded." For the main center span of the ceiling, the boards run north to south, but are reversed, running east to west, for the front and rear sections of the ceiling. The seven main 161 foot steel arches are not visible from the ground floor. The arch outlines in the ceiling are actually North Carolina pine boxing, one inch thick, 8 inch by 12 inch wooden troughs with 55 evenly-spaced circular holes cut in for the hanging lights.

A series of 21 foot long, 8 inch hemlock beams run between the steel arches in the ceiling. The beams overlap, and are bolted together by a steel saddle, which is connected to a hanging threaded rod, fastened to the underside of the steel arch.

The finishing touch of the Auditorium's ceiling is the beautiful tongue and groove wainscoted boards nailed to these planks from the interior. Scaffolding from the iron workers were used to install the ceiling and for any painting. But by climbing around in the attic above the ceiling, carpenters further secured the wainscot boards to each other with random size two by fours and other odd size scrap lumber.

This system of interconnections allows both the wooden ceiling and the seven main steel arches to adjust to strong force winds from a northeaster or hurricane. The parabolic wooden ceiling is indeed a "hanging ceiling." The ceiling was originally the color of unvarnished southern hard pine – yellowish white.

During a fierce storm in late May 1894, when the sides of the building were still open, the driving wind blew the rain on the ceiling and other wood work, causing some of it to warp. The southern pine ceiling suffered considerably during this storm. The damage was quickly repaired by the "skillful artisans" in charge. In the 1980's, when a portion of the ceiling was replaced, an analysis of the old wood revealed a tung oil application rather than a clear varnish or lacquer.

The Carpentry Contract is the longest of the Auditorium contracts, twenty pages in all. The reader is encouraged to read the Carpentry Contract because of the fascinating detail in construction specifications.

Looking to the west - the interior of the Auditorium with all the lights on.

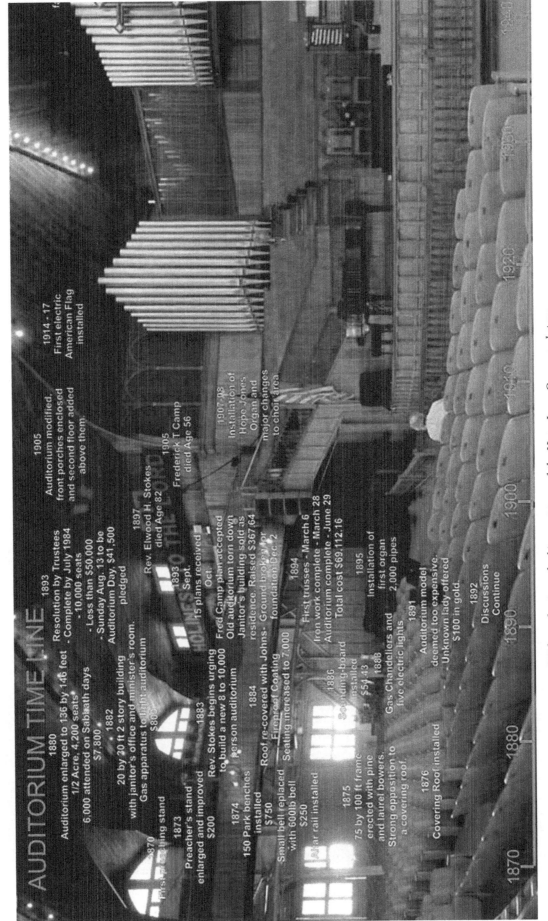

AUDITORIUM TIME LINE

1870
First preaching stand

1873
Preacher's stand enlarged and improved
$200

1874
150 Park benches installed
$750

1875
75 by 100 ft frame erected with pine and laurel bowers.
Strong opposition to a covering roof.

1876
Covering Roof installed

1880
Auditorium enlarged to 136 by 146 feet
1/2 Acre. 4,200 seats
6,000 attended on Sabbath days
$7,800

1882
20 by 20 ft 2 story building with janitor's office and minister's room.
Gas apparatus to light auditorium
$800

1883
Rev. Stokes begins urging to build a new 8 to 10,000 person auditorium

1884
Roof re-covered with Johns-Fireproof Coating
Small bell replaced with 600lb bell
$250
Altar rail installed

Seating increased to 7,000

1886
Sounding board installed
$54.43

1888
Gas Chandeliers and five electric lights

1891
Auditorium model deemed too expensive.
Unknown lady offered $100 in gold.

1892
Discussions Continue

1893
Resolution by Trustees
- Complete by July 1984
- 10,000 seats
- Less than $50,000
- Sunday Aug. 13 to be Auditorium Day. $41,500 pledged

1893
15 plans received Sept.
Oct.
Fred Camp plan accepted
Old auditorium torn down
Janitor's building sold as residence. Raised $367.64
Ground broken for foundation Dec 2

1894
First trusses - March 6
Iron work complete - March 28
Auditorium complete - June 29
Total cost $69,112.16

1895
Installation of first organ
2,000 pipes

1897
Rev. Elwood H. Stokes died Age 82

1905
Frederick T Camp died Age 56

1905
Auditorium modified.
front porches enclosed and second floor added above them

1907-08
Installation of Hope-Jones Organ and major changes to choir area

1914 - 17
First electric American Flag installed

1870 1880 1890 1900 1910 1920 1930

Wide angle view—looking east toward the Hope-Jones Organ and stage.

WAYNE T. BELL, JR. • CINDY L. BELL • DARRELL A. DUFRESNE

1946
Lighted cross added to east face of auditorium in memory of those lost in world war II

1979
Original OCEAN GROVE sign removed from roof

1980
Fire alarm and automatic sprinkler system installed throughout auditorium $277,291

1934 - 1961 - 1969
Many modification made to choir area, central stairway access removed, organ loft expanded and size of choir increased

1986
Original open knob and tube style electrical system modernised to current codes

1994
First Centennial

1999
Choir seats replaced $60,000

2001
16 cluster lights reinstalled around balcony

2004
More restoration of roof, gutters, side-walks and iron finials on the towers

2011
Main tower repair $40,000

1957
Theater seats installed on main floor

1986
A new stainless steel roof coated with non-reflective paint $687,306
this replaced the corrugated aluminum roof which had replaced the original sheet iron

2001
An automatic-electric stage lift installed between the altar rail and the platform

2008
Celebration of 100 years of the Hope Jones organ

1950   1960   1970   1980   1990   2000   2010

Improved Agreement for Building, with Bond.

Articles of Agreement, MADE and entered into this thirteenth

day of January in the year One Thousand, Eight Hundred and Ninety York

Beg and Between LeRoy Hopkins and John B. Roberts constituting

the firm of Hopkins & Roberts

of the City of New York County of

New York and State of New York

as the parties of the first part, hereinafter called the Contractors

2nd the Ocean Grove Camp Meeting Association of the Methodist Episcopal Church of Ocean Grove County of

Monmouth and State of New Jersey

as the party of the second, hereinafter called the Proprietors

Witnesseth, first.—The said parties of the first part do hereby for themselves, thes

heir, executors, administrators or assigns, covenant, promise and agree to and with the said party of of the second

part, their heirs, executors, administrators or assigns, that They the said part die of the first

part Twentieth day of June in the year One Thousand, Eight Hundred

and Ninety York and will and sufficiently erect, finish and deliver in a true, perfect and thoroughly

workmanlike manner, the Carpenter and Sheet metal roofing work

required in the erection and completion of the Auditorium

for the party of the second part, on ground situated in the location of the old Auditorium

in the town of Ocean Grove County of Monmouth

and State of New Jersey agreeably to the Plans, Drawings and Specifications

prepared for the said works by John R. J. Camp Architect, to the satisfaction

and under the direction and personal supervision of said Architect,

and will find and provide such good, proper and sufficient materials, of all kinds whatsoever, as shall be proper and sufficient for the

completing and finishing all the Carpentie and Sheet metal roofing

and other works of the said building as shown by the plans, elevations, sections, details and

signed by the said parties, within the time aforesaid for the sum of Twenty Six Thousand

$26000.00 Dollars

Second.—The said part y of the second part do he hereby for thereflyed heirs, executors, administrators

or assigns, covenant, promise and agree to and with the said part ied of the first part tied their heirs, executors

administrators or assigns, that it of the second part to

and under the direction and personal supervision of said shall, in consideration, of the covenants and agreements being strictly executed,

executors, administrators or assigns, will and shall, in consideration, of the covenants and agreements being strictly executed,

kept and performed by the said part ied of the first part, as specified, well and truly pay, or cause to be paid, unto

the parties of the first part, or unto their heirs, executors, administrators or assigns,

---

SPECIFICATIONS

OF THE MATERIAL AND LABOR TO BE USED AND EMPLOYED IN THE

CARPENTER WORK

of THE AUDITORIUM —

TO BE BUILT FOR

THE OCEAN GROVE C.M. ASS'N

AT

OCEAN GROVE. N.J. —

ACCORDING TO ACCOMPANYING DRAWINGS AND THIS SPECIFICATION,

PREPARED AT THE OFFICE OF

F.T. CAMP. —

ARCHITECT

NEW YORK.

#114 #116 NASSAU ST

3373

The sum of ...Thirty Six thousand... ...Dollars, lawful money of the United States of America, in manner following:

First payment of $.4250... ...when all the timber of the roof is in place...

Second payment of $...1000... ...when metal roofing, &c. ... is in place...

Third payment of $...6750... ...when exterior and interior brickwork, gutters &c.... platform, wall and building ...

Fourth payment of $.4500... ...when work, &c. ... is completed...

Fifth payment of $...3300... ...when...

Sixth payment of $... ...when...

...when the building... ...is all complete, and after the expiration of ...fifteen... ...days, and when all the Drawings and Specifications have been returned to ...Fred K. Camp... ...Architect.

Provided, That in each case of the said payments, a certificate shall be obtained from and signed by ...F. J. Camp... ...Architect... ...to the effect that the work is done in strict accordance with Drawings and Specifications, and that he ...considers the payment properly due; said certificate, however, in no way lessening the total and final responsibility of the Contractor... ...neither shall it exempt the Contractor... from liability to replace work, if it be afterwards discovered to have been done ill, or not according to the Drawings and Specifications, either in execution or materials, and, **Provided further,** that no notice of lien has been served on the Proprietor..., and the Contractor shall show, if required, at the time of making any or final payment by his Affidavit, by Certificate from Clerk of Record Office or by liens, releases or otherwise, as required by law, that the property is free from all liens or claims against the premises or the said Contractor... for work or materials furnished on said works.

AND IT IS HEREBY FURTHER AGREED, BY AND BETWEEN THE SAID PARTIES:

first.—That the Specifications and Drawings are intended to co-operate, so that any works exhibited in the Drawings, and not mentioned in the Specifications, or vice-versa, are to be executed the same as if mentioned in the Specification and set forth in the Drawings, to the true intent and meaning of the said Drawings and Specifications.

Second.—The Contractor... at their... ...own proper cost and charges, to ...once... ...to provide all manner of labor materials, apparatus, scaffolding, utensils and cartage, of every description, needful for the due performance of the several works; must produce, whenever required by Superintendent or Proprietor..., and all vouchers showing the quality of goods and materials used; and render all due and sufficient facilities to the Architect.., Superintendent or Clerk of Works, for the proper inspection of the works and materials, and which are to be under their control; and they may require the Contractor... to dismiss any workman or workmen who they may think incompetent or improper to be employed; the workmen and Contractor being only admitted to the ground for the purpose of the proper execution of the works, and have no tenancy. The Contractor... shall deliver up the works to the Proprietor... in perfect repair, clean and in good condition, when complete. The Contractor... shall not sub-let the works, or any part thereof, without consent in writing of the Proprietor... or Architect...

Third.—Should the Proprietor... at any time during the progress of the said works, require any alterations of, deviations from, additions to, or omissions in the said Contract, Specifications or Plans, he... they... shall have the right and power to make such change or changes, and the same shall in no way injuriously affect or make void the Contract; but the difference for work omitted, shall be deducted from the amount of the Contract, by a fair and reasonable valuation; and for additional work required in alterations, the amount based upon same prices at which contract is taken shall be agreed upon before commencing additions, as provided and hereinafter set forth in Article No. 6; and such agreement shall state also the extension of time (if any) which is to be granted by reason thereof.

fourth.—Should the Contractor..., at any time during the progress of said works, become bankrupt, refuse or neglect to supply a sufficiency of material or of workmen, or cause any unreasonable neglect or suspension of work, or fail or refuse to follow the Drawings and Specifications, or comply with any of the Articles of Agreement, the Proprietor... or his... they... Agent, shall have the right and power to enter upon and take possession of the premises, and may at once terminate the Contract, whereupon all claim of the Contractor..., his... their... executors, administrators or assigns, shall cease; and the Proprietor... may provide materials and workmen sufficient to complete the said works, after giving forty-eight hours' notice, in writing, directed and delivered to the Contractor..., or at his... their... residence or place of business; and the expense of the notice and the completing of the various works will be deducted from the amount of the Contract, or any part of it due, or to become due, to the Contractor...; and in such case no scaffolding or fixed tackle of any kind, belonging to such Contractor..., shall be removed, so long as the same is wanted for the work... But if of the defaulting Contractor..., the same shall belong to the persons legally representing him... them... may have gotten the work completed; but the Proprietor... shall not be liable or accountable to them in any way for the manner in which he... they...

fifth.—Should any dispute arise respecting the true construction or meaning of the Drawings or Specifications, as to what is extra work outside of Contract, the same shall be decided by ...F. J. Camp... his ... ...Architect... and his... ...decision shall be final and conclusive; or in the event of death or unwillingness to act, then of some other known capable Architect, Competent Clerk of Works or Foreman, to be appointed by the Proprietor..., but should any dispute arise respecting the true value of any work, omitted by the Proprietor..., the same shall be valued by two competent persons, one employed by the Proprietor..., and the other by the Contractor..., and these two shall have power to name an umpire, whose decision shall be binding on all parties.

Sixth.—No new work of any description done on the premises, or any work of any kind whatsoever shall be considered as extra unless a separate estimate in writing for the same, before its commencement, shall have been submitted by the Contractor... to the Superintendent and the Proprietor..., and their signatures obtained thereto, and the Contractor... shall demand payment for such work immediately it is done. In case of day's work, statement of the same must be delivered to the Proprietor... at latest during the week following that in which the work may have been done, and only such day's work and extra work will be paid for, as such, as agreed on and authorized in writing.

Seventh.—The Proprietor... will not, in any manner, be answerable or accountable for any loss or damage that shall or may happen to the said works, or any part or parts thereof respectively or for any of the materials or other things used and employed in finishing and completing the said works; or for injury to which might have been prevented by the Contractor..., his... their... workmen, or any one employed by him... them... against all which injuries and damages to persons and property, the Contractor... having control over such work must properly guard against, and must make good all damage from whatever cause, being strictly responsible for the same. Where there are different Contractors employed on the works, each shall be responsible to the other for all damage to work, to persons or property, or for loss caused by neglect, by failure to finish work at proper time and preventing each portion of the works being finished by the several Contractors at date named in this Contract for completion, or from any other cause; and any Contractor suffering damage shall call the attention of the Proprietor... or Superintendent. to the same, for action as laid down in Article No. 4.

Eighth.—The Owner will insure the building... ...in the joint names and interest of himself and the Contractor... against loss or damage by fire in such sums as may from time to time be agreed on with the Contractor... to cover work and materials used in the building and around the premises, and the policies to be made payable to owner and contractor..., as their interest may appear. The Contractor... shall see to it that this insurance is effected to his full satisfaction, and the cost of same will be borne by the Contractor ..., and for any loss of the Contractor... by fire, the owner will not, under any circumstances, be answerable or accountable.

Ninth.—All work and materials, as delivered on the premises to form part of the works, are to be considered the property of the Proprietor..., and are not to be removed without his... their... consent; but the Contractor... shall have the right to remove all surplus materials after his... their... completing the works.

Tenth.—Should the Contractor... fail to finish the work at or before the time agreed upon,............ shall pay to, or allow the Proprietor... by way of liquidated damages, the sum of............... dollars per diem, for each and every day thereafter the said works remain incomplete.

Eleventh.—If any delay is caused by said Proprietor...

In Witness Whereof, the said parties to these presents have hereunto set their names and seals the day and year above written.

Signed, sealed and delivered in the presence of

Witness:

Witness:

S P E C I F I C A T I O N S

of

All the Labor and Materials required in the CARPENTER WORK OF THE AUDITORIUM BUILDING.OCEAN GROVE, N.J.for the OCEAN GROVE CAMP MEETING ASSOCIATION,from plans by F.T.Camp,Architect, No. 114 & 116 Nassau St. N.Y. City.

- - - oo - - -

General Conditions:

The plans and specifications are intended to co-operate, so that a complete and workmanlike job of Carpenter work will be done, and each and everything requisite to so complete said carpenter work according to the intent and meaning of these plans and specifications must be furnished and done,whether specified or drawn or not; and no extras of any kind will be allowed,unless the work is in addition to that comprised herein,and unless a written order for it shall be given by the Architect,with the authority of the building committee. Bidders will state how many working days they will require to execute this contract.

Bonds:

will be required from good and sufficiently responsible real-estate owners,to the amount of half the contract figure,conditioned that if the contractor fully complies with all the requirements of the contract,plans and specifications,then the bonds will not be forfeited;but if the contractor shall not comply with all the aforesaid requirements of contract,plans and specifications,and the Association shall suffer any damage there-from,then said bondsmen shall make good to said Association any and all damage suffered by them on account of the failure of this contractor to strictly comply with all the requirements of the contract,plans and specifications.

IMPROVED
Agreement for Building.
WITH BOND.

BETWEEN

OF THE FIRST PART,
—AND—

OF THE SECOND PART,

Dated _____ 189_

Filed January 19 1894
thes Amuch th

ARCHITECT_____

PALLISER, PALLISER & CO.,
Publishers Fine Architectural Works,
24 E. 42d St., NEW YORK CITY.

Price each, 5 Cents; per dozen, 40 Cents; 40 for $1.00;
100 for $2.00.

BOND.

Know all Men by these Presents. That We

Alexander Wallace and Henry F. Beaton

are ...... jointly and severally ...... held and firmly bound unto the Ocean Grove Camp
Meeting Association,the Methodist Episcopal Church ...... in the sum of .... One Thousand Dollars, Each ......
(8000,) ...... Dollars, for which payment
well and duly to be made, We ...... bind ...... ourselves and each of us ...... our ...... heirs, executors, administrators or assigns.

Whereas the Rev. Hopkins & John G. Roberts ...... have ...... been contracted
with the Ocean Grove Camp Meeting Association,the Methodist Episcopal Church ...... to execute,
construct and complete the Auditorium ...... work, N.J.Metd. Meeting Asc ...... of the New Auditorium
at Ocean Grove, N.J. ...... for the sum of $26,000, et ...... Dollars by a contract
dated January 13th, ... 189 ...... hereunto annexed; and the condition of this obligation is,
that if the said Rev F Hopkins & Roberts ...... shall duly perform
said Contract, and fulfill all the several stipulations therein provided, then this obligation is to be void, but
if otherwise, the same shall be and remain in full force and virtue until ...... We have
by said Association ...... In Witness Whereof, We, We ...... have hereunto set our ...... hand and seal this
13th ...... day of ...... January ...... 1894.

Witnesses:

M Edward f.
D D Smith

Alexander Wallace
Henry F. Beaton

Handrailings

to the four small flights of steps at ends of platform are to be made of the same material and style as the altar rail. In gallery windows and gallery stairs and across one end of porch at Jaintor's office,are to be railings of yellow pine,with 3"x4" base rail,3"x4" hand rail,and 2"x2" balusters,cornered,dressed, and secured to posts,steps,&c in best usual manner,approved and directed by the Architect.

Penn. White Hemlock: All wood called "hemlock" will be "Penn.White Hemlock" Gallery beams,6"x14" front side dressed,front beam of all,6"x16" and 4"x8" braces under same,three sides dressed,and worked and bolted as detailed. Frame the stair wells as shown,with headers and tail beams hung in bridle irons and also spiked. Front stair well and platform leading to it built up over descending platforms,as shown,in strong and workmanlike manner. Bolts for all joints as shown,with large square washers of $\frac{1}{4}$" iron.Ceiling beams of 3"x8",supported by iron slings from steel trusses, and bolted through. N.C. pine boxing,1" thick,and 8"x12" section are to be built down under each truss across ceiling and in front and rear,as shown,and at the sharp curves next walls to die out as shown.Where ceiling beams change direction there must be a sufficient amount of iron straps used as approved by the Architect,furnished by Steel contractor and applied by the Carpenter.Rafter and cross girder supported on steel girders, 8"x10" hemlock,in 4 angle panels of roof,and bolted to steel work with 1" bolts. Bridle irons at framing of cupoles and stair trimming,well fitted and spiked.There will be a stick of undressed hemlock,6"x14" bolted with 1" bolts to 8"x8" framework of the east front,at the line of top of gallery trusses,to support east ends of last panel of gallery floor beams,and at

Timber:

must be square sawn,sound and free from defects,sap or shates, and well seasoned and dressed,where so specified and marked on the drawings,and in the ordinary sawed state where not so marked or specified,and of the different kinds hereafter mentioned.

Yellow Pine:

Main-building sill on sides,rear,and part of front that is open will be 2"x8" with 2"x4"spiked on in center doorways,all dressed and secured to steel columns by angles and lag screws,as per detail. Yellow pine stair carriages,three in number on each flight from galleries to ground,3"x6" dressed,and lower edges chamfered and step blocks of the same spiked on top. These carriages to be lag screwed to header in gallery floor,and to platform timbers, and the carriage next to wall lag screwed to all posts it passes. All posts at platforms and foot of stairs,of dressed and chamfered yellow pine supported on foundations,and all to be framed together with mortise and tenon,and oak pins,in best way and as shown on details. All platform floors and step treads of stairs and to porches,are to be of dressed yellow pine 1 3/8" thick,and laid in strips 3 1/8" wide,and 1/2" open joint between,and two ten penny nails at each bearing,with front and end edges molded half round,and risers are to be 7/8" G.P. dadoed into treads,top and bottom.

Altar Railing:

To be of yellow pine:Newels 4"x4",upper rail 3"x4",lower rail, 3"x5" and 2"x2" turned balusters 5" apart,all as per detail.Sections of this rail at each end are to be made as gates,hung on parliament hinges and provided with strong fastenings as may be approved by the Architect.

Between purlins furnish and set a 3"x10" hemlock stick, supported at ends by cross pieces from purlins of 4"x10" mortised and tenoned, and set rafters at eaves low enough to provide for 2"x4" furring to support metal roofing on 4'0" centers, all well spiked. Eaves projecting 4'0" including gutter are to have a dressed purlin at end of rafters, and secured to them in manner detailed, to support center of purlin, and rafters will be 2"x8", resting on plate, and spiked to second purlin and eaves purlin. Under side of eaves ceiled as provided for in main ceiling. Fur between ceiling beams, 3"x4", three places, and a longitudinal 2"x6", furnished and set, lower side flush. Sheath all roofs,&c. where the Cortright metal slates are to be put, and board valleys with good quality 1" matched and seasoned white pine.

Framing Timber of Front office portion to be undressed hemlock of the following sizes: Sills 4"x6"; studding 3"x4" on 16" centers; plate doubled 2"x4"; floor beams 3"x10",20" centers, and two rows double cross bridging 1½"x3". Jamb studding doubled. Rafters 4"x8" on 12'0" centers with 2"x6" cut between on 4'0" centers in manner similar to mode for main roof, and for same kind of roofing. Ventilating shafts built out of 3"x4" studding,16" centers, from foundation, with a curve in bottom as shown of flooring. Sleepers under platform front and altar railing, of 6" chestnut, bedded in concrete. Platform front of 3"x4" dressed N.C.pine with chamfered corners, and N.C.pine board back, nailed on back. Platform girders 8"x10" hemlock, joined with 2'0" scarf over pier, pinned and resting on brick piers. Platform floor beams 3"x10", on 24" centers, cross bridged twice between girders with 1½"x2½", twice nailed at ends with tens. Altar floor beams 2"x6", on 20" centers. Floor with 1"x3" T&G, N.C.pine. Enclosed parts of main building

each beam there will be spiked a block to keep it vertical. Under this beam at the same distance as bottom line of steel truss there will be bolted in similar manner a 4"x6" dressed hemlock stick, to receive bottom ends of braces.

Front corner Posts of main building will be 8"x8" dressed. Center posts of each panel will be 4"x8" dressed, and the angle braces, only

In front panels and side panel next to front, will be 3"x6" dressed, all mortised and tenoned and secured to steel columns by steel angles and lag screws. Top girt under strut 3"x8" dressed two sides and bolted 4 times to strut as shown, with dressed 3"x8" rebated out and secured upright as detailed. Horizontal girts 6"x8" and 4"x8" dressed 3 sides and the posts will be mortised and tenoned and pinned into them, as detailed, and secured to steel columns by steel angles and lag screws. Furring for closed panels will be 3"x4" dressed 3 sides except for the topmost range behind curved ceiling which will be 2"x3" not dressed. All cutting necessary to allow iron braces to pass these posts, girts and braces, is to be neatly done.

Main Roof Purlins;

Are 8'0" apart on centers, and are to be 4"x12", supported on main trusses, vertical, ends fitted to pitch, and secured to lugs by bolts, and strapped where butting by 2¾" x ¼" x 2'0" iron-strap, 3 holes and 4" wrought iron spikes in each half, and placed on top of purlin. Where purlins do not butt, and these strap cannot be applied, the lugs must be larger and strong enough to stand the strain. Ceiling beams, 3"x8" are directly under these purlins also 8'0" apart, and are connected to them by light truss-sing-braces 3"x4", center hangers 2½"x4", all spiked 4 times each end with 20 penny spikes.

(7)

-ly supported on roof rafters, and braced back to steel truss, which passes through the center of it, and strongly bolted as may be detailed. The outside is cased with 7/8" white pine of a good quality, according to elevation and detail, and cornice of ogee, facia and large cove, bead, &c. and roof is shingled as main roof is, on 2"x6" rafters, resting on 4"x6" plate, tied across strongly and securely and well spiked together. Flashings of all kinds, and in all places required, of painted roofing tin, of best quality, 20" wide, and all valleys must have 4" wider opening at bottom between shingles than at top. All finials are as per design, made of heavy galvanized iron, and supported by large iron rods inside, secured at bottom by long flukes or feet, strongly spiked to principal rafters.

Galvanized Iron Gutters:

Are of main eaves, made of No. 24 iron, 8" wide at top, molded in section, and supported by Berger's irons, and graded so as to throw off water at the points shown, into 6" spiral riveted and soldered No. 24 galvanized iron leaders, which are to be cased with 1¼" yellow pine 7'0" above ground and are to be connected to glazed earthenware drain pipe and bends, which at 3'0" from the walls are to meet the sewers of the Owners. The gutters on the front rooms, offices, &c are to be of the same material as specified for main eaves gutters, but are to be 4" wide on top, and are to be fastened in similar manner and are to have 3" leaders, where shown, and also cased 7'0" above ground, and also to be connected to sewers in best manner. Stamped zinc wreaths over front windows on the front octagon part, selected by Architect.

(8)

and fronts of offices, &c, to be of rebated beveled clapboards 8" wide, best quality, smooth backs, and nailed with cut 6s, and heads well set in. Vertical ceiled parts under eaves of main building and between middle openings and top ones, are of "v" grooved, 6", T&G, 1" matched pine or spruce ceiling, well seasoned.

Metal Roof. Will be made of #26 galvanized corrugated sheet iron of Coe's make, of Newark, 2½" corrugation, with 4" lap at level seams, with paint skin cement in laps, and level laps riveted every corrugation, and 1½" side laps riveted 8" apart, and all nailed to purlins with barbed wire nails, with lead washers. Valleys lined with terne iron sheets, waterproof joints, and sides turned up under corrugated in a water proof manner, and valleys 4" wider at bottom than top. Hips and ridges of #26 galvanized iron, best usual widths, and approved by the Architect. Cortright metal slates of galvanized iron, 7"x10", pattern selected by the Architect, put on all cupola roofs, and the same make, of painted tin, put on all vertical parts of pediments, fronts of small towers, as directed by the Architect. All roofs guaranteed water tight for 5 years.

Cornices: of pediments to main building and porches are of moldings, ogee, facia and quatter round. Cornices of gables of main roof, are fillet, quarter round and facia, all having level ceiled plancer, and friezes of 1¼" pine, in usual manner and as shown. The triangular ventilating dormers on sides are framed on top of roof, in a strong manner, valleys flashed with painted leaded sheet-iron, and roofs covered as main roofs are. Main roof gables are furred and shingled in panels with #1 sawed cedar 18" stock, on shingle lath, in best usual manner, with 1½" panelling in front, with small louvre frames in, as shown, and the rear one is also furred, and clapboarded as before specified. All louvre boards are 1½" pine, cornices as on main roof gables, and space under dormer roofs open for ventilation. Tops of ventilating turrets are cut into octagon at cornice, with broaches tinned and painted, are built of studding, sheathed inside, metal shingled on curves, with pine sill course, outside casing, louvre frames and boards, cornices, rafters, metal shingle roofs, galvanized iron finials on iron rods, per elevations, details and approved by Architect. Rear ridge ventilating turret constructed in same way as front one, except interior sheathing. Main roof front cupola is constructed of 6"x 6" strong angle posts, and 2"x6" studding, on 4"x6" sill, strong-

(8)

Sash:

In main building walls are to fit between posts,and the tops of the openings at posts and lintels are to have filling pieces to make them of gothic shape,as shown. Sash are to be made of 2" good quality white pine,with bars,and glazed with XX American sheet glass,1st quality,well tacked,bedded and puttied. They are not intended to open and close,and are to be securely fastened in,but in such a manner as to be easily taken out.

Window Frames

of front offices are made in the usual manner,for 1½" sliding sash,with pockets,iron weights,2" steel axle pulleys,braided hemp Samson cord,XX American sheet glass,1st quality,berlin-bronze Ives sash fasts,and with two rebated sash lifts in each lower rail. Door frames of outside doors of 1½" jambs,2" sills, and rebated for 2" doors. All outside door and window casings, corner boards,friezes,watertable,&c are to be a good quality 1½" white pine,with weather drips over windows. Interior doors to have 7/8" jambs,and ½"x1½" door stops nailed in. Outside doors raised molded on outside,and flush molded on inside,hung on 3 plain iron japanned butts to each door,and trimmed with flush top and bottom brass face bolts for fast leaf,and good brass face and strike mortise lock and latch,steel keys,and berlin-bronze knobs,plain escutcheons and roses. Interior doors to have 4 panels,the upper two vertical,and the lower two horizontal,and hung on two japanned iron butts and trimmed with brass face and strike lock and latch,and Jet knobs and japanned roses and es-cutcheons,steel keys. Closet doors,rim locks,and knobs only on outside,and closets to have two rows double cast iron japanned clothes hooks,on cleats,and two shelves,as directed by Architect.

(9)

Interior Trim:

of offices and rooms to consist of a good quality of N.C.pine, 7/8"x4½" molded and with wall member,plinths and corner blocks, bases 7/8"x8" open,and molded 1½"x2½". Window trim to finish on stools and aprons. Cellar windows to be of the sizes shown and figured,and to be made of 2" dressed hemlock plank,in usual man-ner to place in brick wall,and sash are to be 1½" thick,glazed with common glass,hung at top with hinges,and provided with hooks to fasten open,and buttons or bolts to fasten shut. Ceil with common 5/8" N.C.pine under side of beams over cellar where fan motor is,and pack between beams full with mill shavings. Ceiling partition around stairs to cellar,and also in Ladies' toilet room,and in cellar enclosing machinery from passage,to be 7/8"x3",double surfaced,beaded,T&G,white pine of a good quality. In cellar and around cellar stairs it will be the whole hight from floor to ceiling,and is to have dadoed strip top and bottom and a quarter round to cover joint. In toilet room it is to be 7'0" high,capped,and the door opening in same neatly trimmed. This door to be a dwarf screen door,in 4 panels,all filled with stationary slats,and to be 1 1/8" thick,and hung on two brass Gem spring hinges and to fasten shut by a spring catch. All doors to have hard wood saddles,neatly fitted and secured to floor.L Carpenter will put up N.C.pine 7/8"x2½" cleats for the wash basin brackets as directed,in Ladies' toilet room.

Flooring:

(Rt gallery floor yellow laten) For platform and galleries to be 1 1/8"x3" N.C.pine,T&G and blind nailed,butts perfectly jointed and bradded and smoothed of immediately after laying. At pulpit lay a square,13'0"x13'0" of old boards from old building. For altar in front of platform,

in that panel, next to steel column, and this door, bearing the sliding door will slide up, thus opening all the 4 spaces in each panel. Steel contractor puts up one channel iron on steel column, and Carpenter the others. Doors will have 1½" glazed sash as shown on detail. Sliding doors to have 5" rolling sheaves, iron track and iron clips at top to hold in place, and the sliding-up doors two strong pulleys, and best t: iron weights, and strong rope, sufficient to do the work, and iron bolts to fasten open, and to fasten shut, and the other sliding doors, similar attachment of hardware, as may be later directed by the Architect. The sliding doors in topmost ranges are made in a similar manner, and roll ro sides on 5" sheaves and iron track as before specified. The second or middle range will be hinged at top with the strongest strap hinges each, and will swing up open, to soffit of gallery. These will be opened and shut by proper ropes and pulleys and other hardware selected by the Architect. Box the weights of the sliding-up doors, and box in these doors above rear gallery floor with 7/8" N.C.pine.

Auditorium:

This word on main pediment to be made in wood letters, according to detail, and strongly secured to face of wall, as may be further directed by the Architect.

No Templates: Furnished by Steel Contractor.

Portage of mason will be made from boards, the shape and size of foot plates of steel columns, with two holes bored, where the anchor rods are to be, so that mason can set them up in exactly the place the rods must occupy, and correctly build them into the masonry work of foundations.

furnished by architect before beginning

---

same as platform, finishing as a kneeling step, with a riser of 7/8". For front rooms, offices, &c the same quality and kind of flooring 7/8" thick and laid in similar manner. Same kind of floor on 6" chestnut sleepers in cellar toilet room. Ten penny nails used in laying 1 1/8" flooring, and eight penny in 7/8". All this flooring will be a good, medium No.1 N.C. pine, free from defects.

Steps:

From platform to main floor made of 1¼" n,c,pine close strings, 1¼" treads and 7/8" risers. Side steps near platform made with similar parts, and continue up to gallery stair landings. All stair treads inside walls are to be in one piece, N.C.Pine, 1 3/8" thick, and with 2½" round hard wood rail on one side, strongly bracketed. The jib panels from gallery floors to stair strings are to be N.C.pine, in one length, 1 1/8" thick, double surfaced, and 3" wide, T&G and beaded, and well and strongly nailed, and neatly fitted and finished, and are to extend above the gallery step platforms, 4'0" high, as a guard railing, and have 1½" capping molded, and secured as may be directed by the Architect.

Steps in front part of main floor from sill down to inclined surface of floor of N.C.pine, 1½" treads, and 7/8" risers, resting on 4"x4" sleepers of chestnut, bedded in concrete. Ceil, inside, and main hall side, of small flights, leading to galleries from altar, with 5/8"x3" T&G N.C.pine.

Doors to all openings in Main Building:

Made of 7/8" x3" double surfaced sound white pine, only small red knots allowed, T&G and beaded, clinch nailed or screwed on to 7/8" x 5" pine frames, rails and braces as per details. On the lowest row the center doors will slide towards and onto the side doors

Ladder to Loft:

Will be made,inclosed,in front corner of south gallery,in a strong and durable manner,with door at bottom,hung and trimmed with suitable hardware,as selected by the Architect;and a path of strong flooring is to be put down,leading to cupola,2'6" wide. Strong ladder to go up in cupola built,and floor cupola with timbers,as detailed,and plank flooring,T&G,and in manner adapted to shed water perfectly,as directed and approved of by Architect.

Gallery Floors:

Will be in steps as shown,with flooring of 1¼" N.C.pine,matched and T&G,and 4" wide,run from top of 6"x14" beam to a flitch spiked on next beam.Ceil bottom of gallery beams on the slope,with 5/8" N.C.pine ceiling of good quality,4" wide,and fill spaces between beams with mill shavings,packed tight,as deafening,as may be further directed by the Architect.

Gallery Fronts:

Will have truss framework of 6"x4" with 1" rods,supported on steel trusses,and ceiled on both sides with N.C.pine ceiling, 5/8" beaded,T&G,and run vertically,and capped with 1¼" N.C. pine,edges molded and well secured to furring,as detailed. The angles at junction of side and rear gallery fronts are to be rounded,on the outside,to the radii figured on the plan. Steps are to be built across angle of platforms in rear part of gallery,see plan.Partitions of 1¼" double surfaces N.C.pine ceiling T&G,and beaded,are to be built as railings at stair wells in gallery,and are to be part of the jib panels of the stairs,and are to be firmly braced,and capped neatly as detailed.

(12)

Cover for Area of Boiler Room.

To be made over same,the roof as now shown,resting on coping of wall,and having in it three hot bed sash skylights,hinged and trimmed with hardware to keep open and fasten shut.Glass protected by ½" mesh,#19 wire,galvanized netting.Roof tinned with before mentioned best quality tin and painted two coats. Fence of 3'0" pickets built around this roof,and strongly attached to the woodwork of roof,all as approved and directed by the Architect. To carry frame wall over area opening,furnish and set in place a sill,a 6"x12" yellow pine stick.

Ceiling Sounding Board.

Will be made of 5/8"x4" dressed and matched,T&G,and beaded and well seasoned N.C. pine,straight through,free from any larger than pin knots,and will be blind nailed to ceiling timbers and furrings,and butts well made and bradded. At sharp curves ar furrings,and put securely in place,extra furrings,sufficient to hold the 5/8" stuff in proper curve,as shown.The two an-gle sides of the platform walls each having 7 windows in,will not have the sharp curve down to wall,but the general segment curve will meet wall,as shown,finishing with a neat angle molding. The direction of the ceiling boards will be across the hall mainly,but will be reversed in the front and rear parts. The recesses for windows over galleries,will be furred co-inciding with the heads of these windows,and the same kind of ceiling as specified for main ceiling,and a bead on angle of rib. The sash which are in front curve of this ceiling sounding board,are to be of small size,to accommodate themselves to the curves,and glazed with common glass. Sash to be 1 3/8" thick,in about 9 lights each,and securely fastened in place by screws,and are not intended to open and close.

(14)

Curtains under Rear Gallery:

Will be made in folding style, out of 5/8" double surfaced N.C. pine ceiling, on 5/8" frames, tails and braces, as detailed, and will be arranged to fold up on hinges, by pulleys and ropes, in manner as detailed and directed by the Architect.

Ventilating Ducts, &c.

These will be built circular as nearly as the use of 2"x12" will permit, and will be ~~either constructed up~~ tarred hemlock plank, and of the sections shown on plans and other drawings. They will be held together by galvanized band iron with screw lugs, or by 3/8" round iron, galvanized, twisted together and clinched, about 3'0" apart, and will have joints broken, and will conform to curves shown; and the last section, 5'0" in diameter, will be secured to the iron frame of the fan in a workmanlike manner, as directed by the Architect. Curbs will be built of 2" tarred ~~or pressed~~ plank, affixed to top of ventilating ducts with proper strengthening as may be detailed, and are to extend up 5" to surface, and and are to be fitted to receive the following gratings. These will be 10 in number, about 4'0" x 5'0", or such a size as will allow the aggregate of all the openings in all the 10 gratings to be 80 sq. ft. They are to be made of oak or yellow pine, 1 1/2" x 2 1/2" bars, the narrow way up, halved together, making holes 2"x2", and a deep edge to fit over curb like a scuttle cover. Bars to be screwed together at each intersection.

Attention make before signing.

Attention make before signing.

Sounding Boards:

That in rear of platform is to be constructed of same materials as the ceiling, and on the curves shown on the floor plan, secured to 2"x4" studding furrings, on 16" centers, braced to main walls,

---

(15)

and finished with a neat wooden cornice and cresting, out of 1 1/2" white pine, cut in pattern shown or detailed.

Sounding board placed over Speaker will be constructed of dry, seasoned spruce, in wedge shaped pieces, 7/8"x3", T&G, matched and dressed 2 sides, blind nailed onto curved furrings, and suspended by wire ropes from ceiling timbers. The curves of this sounding board will be detailed, and the size of it will be about 25' wide at top, 15' wide at bottom, and length about 25'.

Ventilator Openings

In ceiling, 8'0"x6'0" between ceiling beams, and will be in panels 10" square, bars dressed 4"x4" hemlock, as cover, a square section of boards, hung on pulleys and wire cord, so it can be raised entirely free from grating, or let down on it, to open and close the same. There will be 4 of these, one under each cupola, and two at equal intervals between.

Scaffolding

will be left up for use of painter for a reasonable time, after Carpenters are done using same.

Bolts, Lag Screws, &c.

Carpenter will use all bolts, lag screws, &c. that are in wood work, and which are to be furnished by steel contractor, as also are all suspender slings, bridle irons, straps, and bolts securing wood to steel, &c. &c.

Safety of Structure.

Contractor for carpenter work will be responsible for all his work and material up to the delivery and acceptance of the building by the Architect, and he must make good any damage by fire or elements, without damage being suffered by the Owners.

No work of any kind must be performed on Sundays.

The lower level seats were temporarily removed in 1993 while the interior woodwork of the Auditorium was refinished. Scaffolding was used to reach the ceiling, and the paneling was removed around the choir loft area, revealing the original wooden railings.

Chapter Six

PAINTING, PLUMBING AND ELECTRIC

There are several newspaper references to local contractors not being included in the bidding contracts. It would appear that the building committee was concerned that the construction of the Auditorium in its various phases was beyond the expertise and experience of local firms. The Camp Meeting had a tight schedule with regard to the opening date of the Auditorium. However, in the interest of local support, three contracts were awarded for painting, plumbing and brick work to local businesses. One subcontract for lumber supplies was awarded to Charles Lewis and Buchanon and Smock, a local lumber company. No data is available on this contract.

Painting

The Articles of Agreement for the staining and painting of the Auditorium building were signed on December 15, 1893, by George Bennett of Ocean Grove. The contract price was $1,545, with the first payment of $800 when all the wood work had received two coats of paint and sheet metal one coat, the second payment of $745 when the painting was entirely completed. Should Bennett fail to finish the work on or before May 15, 1894, he was liable for "the sum of five dollars per diem for each and every day thereafter the said works remain incomplete."

The contract was signed and sealed by George Bennett and E. H. Stokes, President, with Wistar H. Stokes, as witness. Wistar H. Stokes, a nephew of Rev. Stokes, was appointed by the Association as Secretary of the Buildings Committee with instructions to keep proper minutes in the form of a "Day Book, accounts and other needful records and to receive and give receipts for all subscriptions and pay the same over to the Treasurer."

A bond of $1,545 was required and any disputes regarding the painting were to be decided by architect Camp. Specifically, the paint to be used was from three sources: Rubber Paint Company of New York; Dixon Graphite paint for exposed steel, tin and galvanized iron; and Murphy's (of Newark, New Jersey) Stain-filler (or equivalent) for the sounding board ceiling and other wood-work. There is one short reference in the *Ocean Grove Record* to the cooperative use of the carpenters' scaffolding by the painters. The suggested exterior building colors were shades of drab and brown, trimmed with a contrasting color. The exterior letters "Auditorium" were gilded. Three coats were required on all outside surfaces. The steelwork above the ceiling had received two coats of paint by the Milliken Brothers as part of their contract. Presently, the OGCMA schedules painting of one side of the Auditorium (depending upon its condition) about once every five years at a cost of $10,000 - $12,000.

Of note is a description of the color of the ceiling at the time of the August 1894 dedication – "a clear stain, yellowish white in color." Over the next hundred years, the interior yellow pine ceiling aged into a soft patina of golden brown. In 1988, a large area of wainscot around the west ceiling grate was replaced due to severe water leakage from the west tower. Other ceiling areas were also reworked. The OGCMA contracted workers to refinish the entire interior woodwork, including the ceiling span, curved arches, wainscoting on the front walls and stairways, altar rails, etc. This restoration project involved removal of the main floor seats so floor-to-ceiling scaffolding could be assembled. The job was completed during the off-season of 1993.

Plumbing

The plumbing contract was awarded to John S. Flitcroft and Brothers of Ocean Grove, on December 12, 1893, for the sum of $175.00. A bond of $100 was signed by John Flitcroft with a job completion date set for May 15, 1894.

These specifications are less than two pages in length, and other bathroom specifications are discussed in the carpentry contract. Without Camp's original architectural plans, we are unable to determine the original number or placement of bathrooms at the time of the official dedication of the Auditorium in 1894.

The water closets were to be of the best pattern of bowl "wash outs" with a "wooden seat and lid secured to the bowl and supplied with cold water through 1¼ inch D lead pipe from iron cisterns. The cisterns were supplied by a ½ inch A lead pipe from the main (line)," probably from Pilgrim Pathway.

Specifics for the water closet fixtures required a "wash basin of marbled porcelain, set in 1¼ inch marble slab, molded and countersunk, and 1 inch marble molded backs, supplied with water through ½ inch A lead pipe and nickel plated faucet - low and short spout, and plated chain, plug and chain stay." The wash basin was "supported by a neat pattern of fancy bronzed brackets screwed to wooden cleats, screwed to wall by carpenter."

The basins and water closets traps were ventilated by a McClellan trap vent. Water was to be transported "to the boiler room through a 2 inch galvanized iron main, with a stop cock at cellar walls and a 3 inch blow off outlet put in and connected to outlet for this purpose, provided by mason."

The installation of the Hope-Jones organ in 1907-1908 required major alterations to the front (east) end of the Auditorium and the choir loft. The east façade of the building was extended out approximately 20 feet. A second story was added, closing in the eight colored-glass windows and the lower half of the two small towers. Two of the original water closets accessible by a small stairs were relocated at that time to the north east side of the building.

Before the new Youth Temple was constructed in 1999 a large comfort station was built across from the Auditorium on Pilgrim Pathway. This provided much needed modern facilities for the large audiences attending the Auditorium programs, and was incorporated into the larger Youth Temple structure.

In 1980 an automatic air pressure sprinkler system was installed throughout the Auditorium, to protect the wooden structure in case of fire. This sprinkler system operates on the principle of constant air pressure, as there is no water in the pipes. This way, pipes will not burst during the winter months because the Auditorium remains unheated throughout the year. With careful examination, the astute observer can spot the sprinkler heads under the balcony or in the ceiling.

Electric

As Ocean Grove grew from a summer tent colony to a year round community it was necessary to provide water, gas, sewer, telephone, telegraph and electric services to attract visitors and

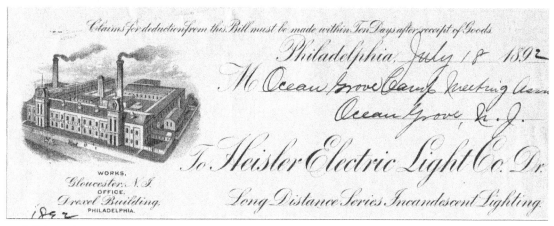

A bill from the Heisler Electric Light Company dated July 18, 1892.

lot purchasers. The trustees were sensible visionaries and planned accordingly. In 1888, a brick building 22 feet by 49½ feet was erected at the North End to house a generator system. This system provided power for both lights and the pumping of water from Association wells.

Within a few years, the electric system supplied power to some 407 lamps on 386 street poles over 22 miles of wire. Eventually, the existing direct-current Heisler system was converted to a Westinghouse alternating current system with carbon Edison light bulbs. New equipment such as a Bass Corliss engine was installed in the power house in 1895 at a cost of $14,944.82. With such an investment in the Auditorium, it was absolutely imperative that an efficient lighting system be available and that it function properly.

The previous Auditorium was illuminated by kerosene lamps and a gas/coal generator system. Brighter lights were needed to light this new huge space, particularly at night. The electri-

The bulb on a flexible cord hangs below the hole cut in the wooden arch. This sample light bulb is on display in the Historical Society Museum.

cal contract is especially timely when placed in the context of the emerging electric lighting systems of the late nineteenth century and the date of signing.

The contract for the wiring and installation of 800 lights in the Auditorium was signed on May 5, 1894, by Field and Hoffman, Electrical Engineers and Contractors, Bible House – New York, at a bid price of $1,248.00, work to be finished on or before June 16, 1894. Field and Hoffman had only 40 days to install the system.

The address of Field and Hoffman, electrical contractors, is most interesting. Bible House, New York, was actually a six-story brick office building on Third and Fourth Avenues from Eighth to Ninth Street opposite Astor Place and was the headquarters of the American Bible Society. Many offices were rented to various firms by the Bible Society. This address might be considered as tacit endorsement by the American Bible Society of a firm's reliability to the public.

The contract called for Field & Hoffman to furnish and install across "the ceiling span 405 cut-outs fused double pole 405 Edison keyless sockets." Each of the seven arches contains 55 lights, a number that many congregants can attest to, as they sit counting light bulbs during lengthy sermons.

Lighting in the arches at the Roosevelt University Auditorium Theatre in Chicago.

The light bulb is pulled up through the hole in the wooden trough. An inquisitive English sparrow watches the procedure.

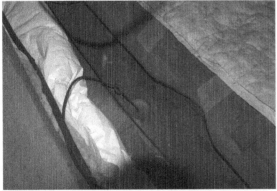

With the bulb hanging about 18 inches below the wooden arch, a simple knot and a round copper plate secure it in place.

The arch lights and the method of bulb replacement are simple. A similar but not exact system was introduced during 1886-1889 in Chicago, Illinois, at the now Auditorium Theatre of Roosevelt University. The specifications for this Auditorium Theatre are 118' wide by 246' long, 4,200 seats and 3,500 clear glass carbon filament bulbs. The architects were Louis Sullivan and Dankmar Adler. While no evidence exists of a direct connection between the Chicago architects and New York architect Frederick Camp, the similarity of the two structures and the arch lighting system suggests that Camp's design may have been influenced by Sullivan and Adler.

Originally the bulbs were early MAZDA W-520 bulbs developed by the Edison Electric Company. By the mid 1980s, many light bulbs hung unlit from the Auditorium ceiling spans. A campaign, "Light the Light," headed by Dr. George "Doc" Stoll (1913-2008) was begun to fund the upgrade and rewiring of the original knob and tube electrical system. The bulbs currently in use provide 525 lumens at 66 watts. This allows some 14,000 hours of light output and cuts down on maintenance service to the bulbs.

A system of electric wires and boxes provides service to the bulbs as they hang some 18 inches below each wooden arch in the ceiling. Replacement of a burned out bulb is easily accomplished from a catwalk above the overhead ceiling, by pulling a flexible cord that lifts the light bulb up through a two-inch circular hole in the wooden arch. The angle trusses are similarly lighted for a total of 1,148 incandescent lamps with a total candlepower (C.P.) of 16,304 watts.

Originally, 24 brass cluster light fixtures, each with five bulbs, hung around the perimeter of the Auditorium, both on and under the balcony. These polished brass clusters were specially made with canopies to cover the fuses. Over the years, these light fixtures were removed, but 16 cluster light fixtures were reinstalled around the balcony in 2001.

Two lighted signs are among the Auditorium's most distinctive features and may be the oldest

These two lighted signs "HOLINESS TO THE LORD" and "SO BE YE HOLY" are the mottos of the Holiness movement

operating electric signs in America. Measuring roughly 4 feet by 32 feet, they are constructed of sheet metal, in a frame, with small holes punched through for the light bulbs. The first sign, installed in 1894 in the center over the choir loft, proclaimed "*Holiness To The Lord,*" a most appropriate statement of the theological viewpoint of the Holiness founders of Ocean Grove. When the first organ from Washington Square Church in NYC was installed in 1895, the center organ pipes blocked the sign. The sign was shifted to the north, still over the choir loft. To provide balance, a second sign declaring "*So Be Ye Holy*" was installed on the south side above the choir loft. With the installation of the Hope-Jones organ in 1907-1908, both signs were moved yet again, this time to the balcony level, on the eastern walls, where they remain to this day. These two signs retained their original knob and tube wiring system until recently, when they were rewired to code.

Restoration Ball Chairperson Beth Gannon and Auditorium Employee Al Wanamaker hold one of the 16 new brass sconces. These five bulb fixtures are replicas of original lighting attached to the gallery fascia.

Early interior postcard photos provide evidence of other electrical items. For example, at various times lighted crosses have decorated the front of the Auditorium - a small red cross with crown (which now hangs in the OGCMA office) and another simple larger cross measuring approximately 6 feet in height.

Perhaps the most unusual fixture in the Auditorium is the electric American flag, located directly in the front center. Built sometime between 1914 and 1917, it replaced hanging cloth flags. The wooden flag measured 10 feet by 18 feet and has a sequential flickering light system such that the flag appears to be waving. This flag is lit when the *National Anthem* is sung, and especially when John Philip Sousa's

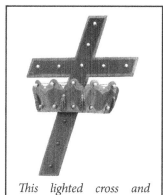

This lighted cross and crown is now displayed at the OGCMA office.

great march *Stars and Stripes, Forever* is played in the Auditorium. It is an intense patriotic scene when a crowd of 4,000 to 6,000 people clap and shout for "Old Glory." A new, updated three-part fiberglass flag was installed in 2004 to replace the heavier wooden model. For Sunday services, with the exception of July 4, this flag is lowered behind the choir loft, exposing a gold and brown Gothic cross. The former retired flag is being refurbished at the Neptune High School and will be displayed at the new Performing Arts Center at the school.

The original wooden American Flag (10 feet by 18 feet) with sequential flashing lights that resembled a flag waving in the breeze.

The exterior lighting for the Auditorium was originally "goose-neck" lights with rounded green shades. This lighting was replaced in 1986 with outdoor spotlights. Outside on the main tower hangs a sheet metal cross with fluorescent tubes that can be seen for 15 miles out to sea. Although we don't know the exact date that an original wooden cross was installed on the main tower, there is a notation in the 1945 *Ocean Grove Record* that an electric cross was installed that summer to replace the wooden one. This cross was then replaced, believe it or not, by movie director Woody Allen. While filming *Stardust Memories* in Ocean Grove in 1980, Allen used the front of the Auditorium as a Victorian hotel. The cross was removed by Allen for the film shooting, and replaced with a new model after the film was complete.

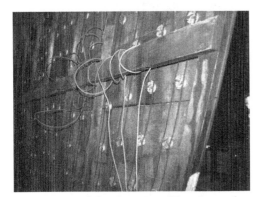

Rear view of the American Flag shows the lamp sockets and wiring.

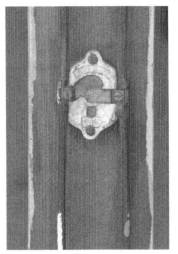

A ceramic fuse attached to the woodwork of the Flag.

The huge electric cross on the front tower can be seen for 15 miles at sea.

Painting Contract

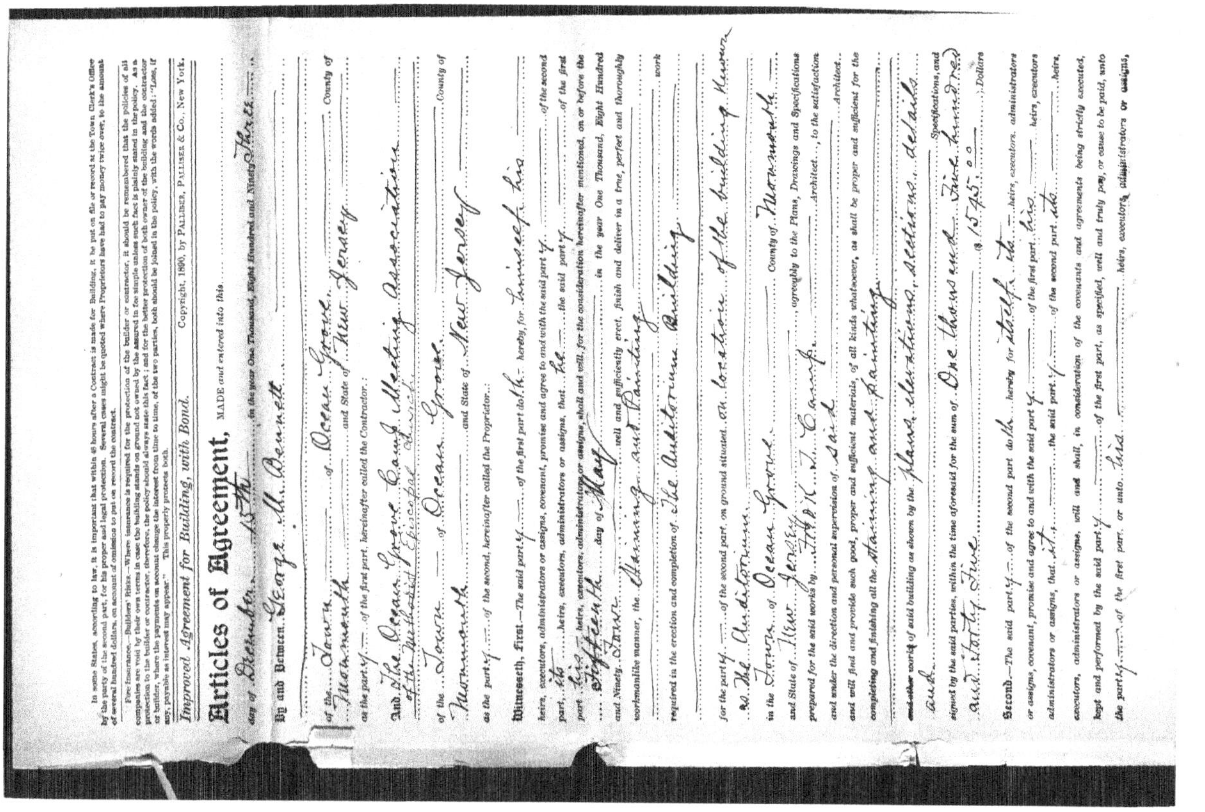

In some States, according to law, it is important that within 48 hours after a Contract is made for Building, it be put on file or record at the Town Clerk's Office by the party of the second part, for his proper and legal protection. Several cases might be quoted where Proprietors have had to pay money twice over, to the amount of several hundred dollars, on account of omission to put on record the contract.

Fire Insurance.—Builders' Risks.—Where insurance is required for the protection of the builder or contractor, it should be remembered that the policies of all companies are void by their own terms in case the building stands on ground not owned by the assured in fee simple unless such fact is plainly stated in the policy. As a protection to the builder or contractor, therefore, the policy should always state this fact; and for the better protection of both owner of the building and the contractor or builder, where the payments on account change the interest from time to time, of the two parties, both should be joined in the policy, with the words added: "Loss, if any, payable as interest may appear." This properly protects both.

Improved Agreement for Building, with Bond. Copyright, 1890, by Palliser, Palliser & Co., New York.

Articles of Agreement, MADE and entered into this day of December 15th in the year One Thousand, Eight Hundred and Ninety Three

By and Between George M. Bennett

of the Town of Ocean Grove County of Monmouth and State of New Jersey

as the party of the first part, hereinafter called the Contractor:

And The Ocean Grove Camp Meeting Association of the Methodist Episcopal Church

of the Town of Ocean Grove County of Monmouth and State of New Jersey

as the party of the second, hereinafter called the Proprietor.:

Witnesseth, First.—The said party of the first part doth hereby, for himself his heirs, executors, administrators or assigns, covenant, promise and agree to and with the said party of the second part, its heirs, executors, administrators or assigns, that he the said party of the first part his heirs, executors, administrators or assigns, shall and will, for the consideration hereinafter mentioned, on or before the Fifteenth day of May in the year One Thousand, Eight Hundred and Ninety Four well and sufficiently erect, finish and deliver in a true, perfect and thoroughly workmanlike manner, the Staining and Painting work required in the erection and completion of The Auditorium Building

for the party of the second part, on ground situated on location of the building known as the Auditorium in the Town of Ocean Grove County of Monmouth and State of New Jersey, agreeably to the Plans, Drawings and Specifications prepared for the said works by Frank T. Camp Architect, to the satisfaction and under the direction and personal supervision of said Architect, and will find and provide such good, proper and sufficient materials, of all kinds whatsoever, as shall be proper and sufficient for the completing and finishing all the staining and painting ~~and other~~ work of said building as shown by the plans, elevations, sections, details and Specifications, and signed by the said parties, within the time aforesaid for the sum of One thousand Five hundred and Forty Five ($1545.00) Dollars

Second.—The said party of the second part doth hereby for itself its heirs, executors, administrators or assigns, covenant, promise and agree to and with the said party of the first part his heirs, executors, administrators or assigns, that it the said party of the second part its heirs, executors, administrators or assigns, will and shall, in consideration of the covenants and agreements being strictly executed, kept and performed by the said party of the first part, as specified, well and truly pay, or cause to be paid, unto the party of the first part, or unto his heirs, executors, administrators or assigns,

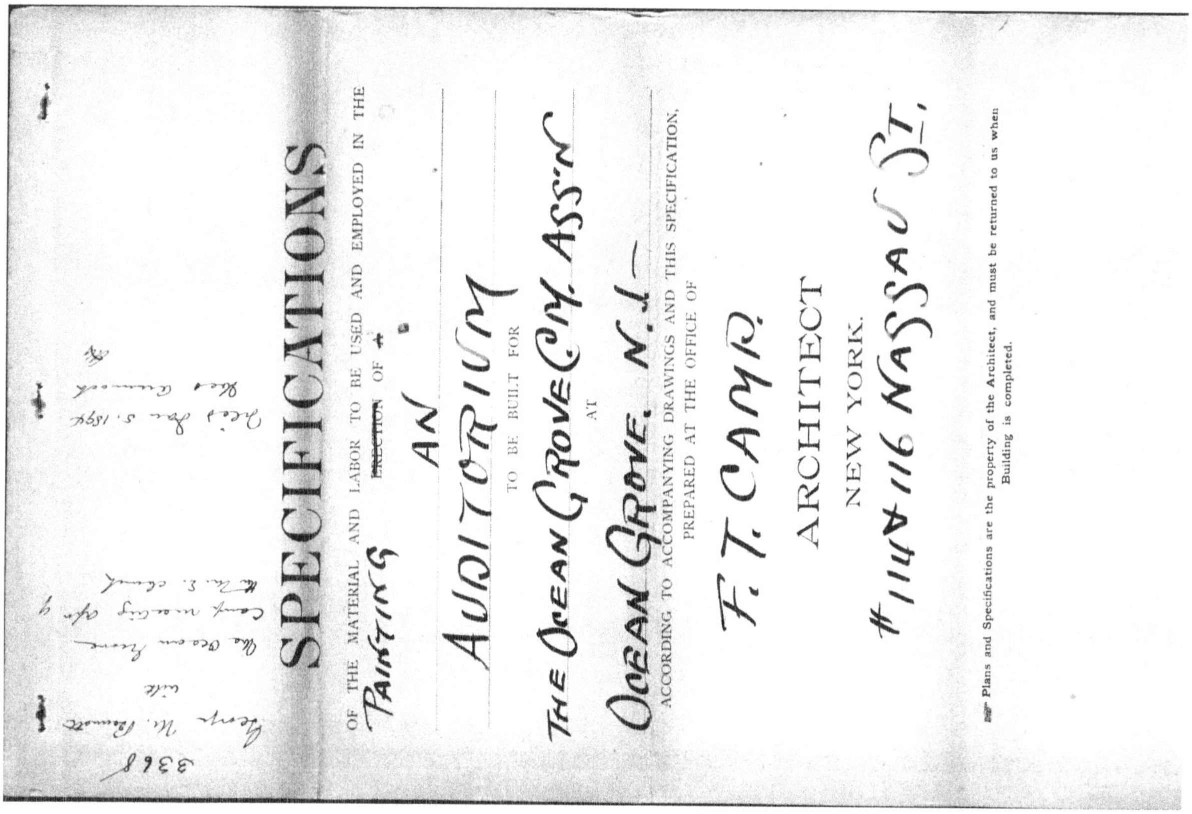

3368

Geo. M. Bennett

with

The Ocean Grove Camp meeting Assn of the M. E. church

Rec'd Jan 5. 1894

Geo. Bennett

SPECIFICATIONS

OF THE MATERIAL AND LABOR TO BE USED AND EMPLOYED IN THE PAINTING ~~ERECTION~~ OF AN AUDITORIUM

TO BE BUILT FOR

THE OCEAN GROVE C. M. ASS'N

AT

OCEAN GROVE. N. J.—

ACCORDING TO ACCOMPANYING DRAWINGS AND THIS SPECIFICATION, PREPARED AT THE OFFICE OF

F. T. CAMP.

ARCHITECT

NEW YORK.

#114 & 116 NASSAU ST.

Plans and Specifications are the property of the Architect, and must be returned to us when Building is completed.

The sum of *One Thousand Two Hundred and Forty five* — *$45.00* ....dollars, lawful money of the United States of America, in manner following:

First payment of $ *8.00.* ......when *all work N.E K. Kate removed Fire* .... Credit of paint + Clerk. metal heat ....when .. * Extra'd complete.*

Second payment of $ *745.* ....when.. *Extra'd. complete.*

Third payment of $ ....when.. ....

Fourth payment of $ ....when.. ....

Fifth payment of $ ....when.. ....

Sixth payment of $ ....when.. ....

................is all complete, and after the expiration of *Fifteen*........days, and when all the Drawings and Specifications have been returned to.. *F.E.K. Cauly* ......Architect.

J. F. Dauly, That in each case of the said payments, a certificate shall be obtained from and signed by ....Architect.. ...to the effect that the work is done in strict accordance with *Drawings and Specifications, and that he*..........considers the payment properly due; said certificate, however, in no way lessening the total and final responsibility of the Contractor...; neither shall it exempt the Contractor.. ..from liability to replace work, if it be afterwards discovered to have been done ill, or not according to the Drawings and Specifications, either in execution or materials, and, *Provided further, that no notice of lien has been served on the Proprietor.., and the Contractor shall show, if required, at the time of making any or final payment by his Affidavit, by Certificate from Clerk of Record Office or by lien, releases or otherwise, as required by lien law, that the property is free from all liens or claims against the premises or the said Contractor.. ..for work or materials furnished on said works.*

AND IT IS HEREBY FURTHER AGREED, BY AND BETWEEN THE SAID PARTIES:

First.—That the Specifications and Drawings are intended to co-operate, so that any works exhibited in the Drawings, and not mentioned in the Specifications, or vice-versa, are to be executed the same as if mentioned in the Specification and set forth in the Drawings, to the true intent and meaning of the said Drawings and Specifications.

Second.—The Contractor.. at his *own proper cost and charges, is* ....to provide all ....*right of Norti. s.* ....*by* ......*by* ......*own proper cost and charges, is* ....to provide all manner of labor materials, apparatus, scaffolding, utensils and cartage, of every description, needful for the due performance of the several works; must produce, whenever required by Superintendent or Proprietor.., all vouchers showing the quality of goods and materials used; and render all due and sufficient facilities to the Architect.., Superintendent or Clerk of Works, for the proper inspection of the works and materials, and which are to be under their control; and they may require the Contractor to dismiss any workman or workmen who they may think incompetent or improper to be employed; the workmen and Contractor being only admitted to the ground for the purpose of the proper execution of the works, and have no tenancy. The Contractor.. shall deliver up the works to the Proprietor.. in perfect repair, clean and in good condition, when complete. The Contractor.. shall not sub-let the works, nor any part thereof, without consent in writing of the Proprietor.. or Architect..

Third.—Should the Proprietor.. at any time during the progress of the said works, require any alterations of, deviations from, additions to, or omissions in the said Contract, Specifications or Plans, he.............. shall have the right and power to make such change or changes, and the same shall in no way injuriously affect or make void the Contract; but the difference for work omitted, shall be deducted from the amount of the Contract, by a fair and reasonable valuation; and for additional work required in alterations, the amount based upon same prices at which contract is taken shall be agreed upon before commencing additions, as provided and hereinafter set forth in Article No. 6; and such agreement shall state also the extension of time (if any) which is to be granted by reason thereof.

---

fourth.—Should the Contractor.. at any time during the progress of said works, become bankrupt, refuse or neglect to supply a sufficiency of material or of workmen, or cause any unreasonable neglect of suspension of work, or fail or refuse to follow the Drawings and Specifications, or comply with any of the Articles of Agreement, the Proprietor.. or his.. ......Agent, shall have the right and power to enter upon and take possession of the premises, and may at once terminate the Contract, whereupon all claim of the Contractor.., his.. ..executors, administrators or assigns, shall cease; and the Proprietor.. may provide materials and workman sufficient to complete the said works, after giving forty-eight hours' notice, in writing, directed and delivered to the Contractor.. or at his.. ......residence or place of business; and the expense of the notice and the completing of the various works will be deducted from the amount of the Contract, or any part of is due, or to become due, to the Contractor.. ; and in such case no scaffolding or fixed tackle of any kind, belonging to the Contractor.. , the same shall belong to the persons legally representing him...............but the Proprietor.. shall not be liable or accountable to them in any way for the manner in which he.............. may have gotten the work completed.

fifth.—Should any dispute arise respecting the true construction or meaning of the Drawings or Specification.., as to what is extra work outside of Contract, the same shall be decided by.. *F. V.* *Cauly* ....Architect.. and his.. .....decision shall be final and conclusive; or in the event of his.. ......death or unwillingness to act, then of some other known capable Architect, Competent Clerk of Works or Foreman, to be appointed by the Proprietor.. the same shall be valued by two competent persons, of any.. *four* ..., omitted by the Contractor.. , and the other by the Contractor.. , and these two shall have power to name one employed by the Proprietor.. , and the other by the Contractor.. , and these two shall have power to name an umpire, whose decision shall be binding on all parties.

Sixth.—No new work of any description done on the premises, or any work of any kind whatsoever shall be considered as extra unless a separate estimate in writing for the same, before its commencement, shall have been submitted by the Contractor.. to the Superintendent and the Proprietor.. , and their signatures obtained thereto, and the Contractor.. shall demand payment for such work immediately it is done. In case of day's work, statement of the same must be delivered to the Proprietor at latest during the week following; that in which the work may have been done, and only such day's work and extra work will be paid for, as such, as agreed on and authorized in writing.

Seventh.—The Proprietor.. will not, in any manner, be answerable or accountable for any loss or damage that shall or may happen to the said works, or any part or parts thereof respectively or for any of the materials or other things used and employed in finishing and completing the said works; or for injury to any person or persons, either workmen or the public, or for damage to adjoining property, from any cause which might have been prevented by the Contractor.. , his.. ......workmen, or any one employed by him.....against all which injuries and damages to persons and property, the Contractor..having control over such work must properly guard against, and must make good all damage from whatever cause, being strictly responsible for the same. Where there are different Contractors employed on the works, each shall be responsible to the other for all damage to work, to persons or property, or for loss caused by neglect, by failure to finish work at proper time and preventing each portion of the works being finished by the several Contractors at date named in this Contract for completion, or from any other cause; and any Contractor suffering damage shall call the attention of the Proprietor.. or Superintendent.. to the same, for action as laid down in Article No. 4.

Eighth.—The Owner will insure the building...........in the joint names and interest of himself and the Contractor..against loss or damage by fire in such sums as may from time to time be agreed on with the Contractor..to cover work and materials used in the building and around the premises, and the policies to be made payable to owner and contractor.. as their interest may appear. The Contractor.. shall see to it that this insurance is effected to his full satisfaction, and the cost of same will be borne by the Contractor.. , and for any loss of the Contractor.. by fire, the owner will not, under any circumstances, be answerable or accountable.

Ninth.—All work and materials, as delivered on the premises to form part of the works, are to be considered the property of the Proprietor.. , and are not to be removed without his.. ......consent; but the Contractor.. shall have the right to remove all surplus materials after his.. ......completing the works.

Tenth.—Should the Contractor.. fail to finish the work at or before the time agreed upon,...........shall pay to, or allow the Proprietor.. by way of liquidated damages, the sum of.. *F. V.* .... dollars per diem, for each and every day thereafter the said works remain incomplete.

Eleventh.—

In Witness Whereof, the said parties to these presents have hereunto set their names and seals

the day and year above written.

Signed, sealed and delivered in the presence of

Witness: *Wistar Holster* _____ *Geo W Bennett* Part.. of the First Part.

Witness: *Wabar Notter* _____ *E. W. Notter* Part.. of the Second Part. Prest.

S P E C I F I C A T I O N S

—for the—

Labor and Materials required in doing the Painting of the Auditor-
ium Building, Ocean Grove, N. J. for the Ocean Grove Camp Meeting
Association, from plans made by F. T. CAMP, Architect, No. 114
Nassau Street, N. Y. City.

————oo0oo————

Conditions:

The plans and specifications are intended to
co-operate, so that a finished and workmanlike job of painting will be done, and each and everything requisite to so
finish and complete the painting work according to the intent
and meaning of these plans and specifications must be furnished and done, whether it is so specified, or drawn, or not,
and no extras of any kind will be allowed, unless the work is
in addition to that comprised herein, and unless a written
order for it shall be given by the Architect, with the
authority of the Building Committee. Bidders will state how
many working days they require to complete work. The paint
to be used will be made by the "Rubber Paint Company of New
York", and will be in shades of drab and brown, trimmed with
a contrasting color, to be hereafter decided, as these colors
are merely suggestive.

There will be 3 coats on all outside work, cornices,
eave soffits, posts, railings, trim corner boards, watertable
&c. On all tin, galvanized iron, and exposed steel work there
will be one-coat Dixon's Graphite paint, in some shade hereafter selected. No steel work that is above the ceiling is to
painted in this contract, as it has already had two coats by

Geo. M. Bennett.

IMPROVED
Agreement for Building.
WITH BOND.

BETWEEN

*Geo M Bennett
Painting*

OF THE FIRST PART,

—AND—

*Ocean Grove Camp
Meeting Association*

OF THE SECOND PART,

Dated *Dec. 15th* 1893

Filed 189

ARCHITECT,

F. T. Camp.
114 & 116 Nassau St. N.Y

PALLISER, PALLISER & CO.,
Publishers Fine Architectural Works,
24 E. 42d St., NEW YORK CITY.

Price each, 5 Cents; per dozen, 40 Cents; 40 for $1.00;
100 for $2.00.

BOND. *J. Geo. M. Bennett*

Know all Men by these Presents. That *I. Geo. M. Bennett*

Witnesses:

Geo. M Bennett

Steel Contractor.

All interior wood work in front rooms, to be filled with a stain-filler, and have two coats of best interior varnish, as good as Murphy's of Newark.

Woodwork of front of platform, altar and stair railings, front of gallery, cornice of rear of platform sounding board, also all parts of the enclosed panels of outside walls which are at any time visible to the eye and the inside of all sash and doors, are to have 3 coats paint, in tints as may be directed. The main ceiling sounding board, and that at rear of platform and over Speaker are to be stain filled only, 1 coat. The under side of galleries to have 2 coats. Cellar sash 2 coats inside and 3 out, and woodwork in cellar, 2 coats of light gray. Finials gilded on tips and balls, and vane and letters, "Auditorium" gilded. Separate figure on painting all roofs.

Plumbing Contract

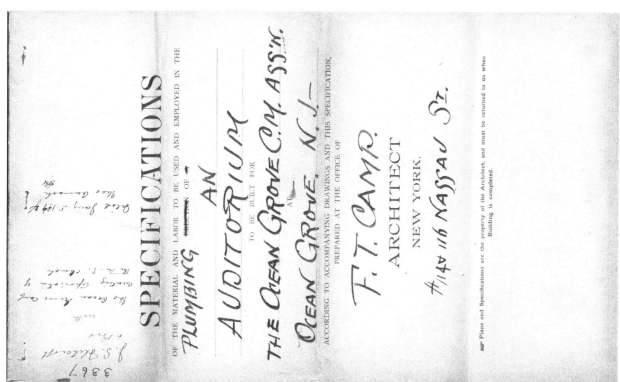

The sum of One Hundred and Seventy-Five @ 175.00 ...Dollars, lawful money of the United States of America, in manner following:

First payment of $...175.00....when....
Second payment of $..............when....
Third payment of $..............when....
Fourth payment of $..............when....
Fifth payment of $..............when....
Sixth payment of $..............when....

....when the building........is all complete, and after the expiration of ....fifteen........days, and when all the Drawings and Specifications have been returned to ....Fred M. J. Camp........Architect....

Proviso, That in each case of the said payments, a certificate shall be obtained from and signed by ....Fred M. J. Camp...........Architect....to the effect that the work is done in strict accordance with Drawings and Specifications, and that he....considers the payment properly due; said certificate, however, is no way lessening the total cost and responsibility of the Contractor....from liability to replace work, if it be afterwards discovered to have been done ill, or not according to the Drawings and Specifications, either in execution or materials, and, Provided further, that no notice of lien has been served on the Proprietor..., and the Contractor shall show, if required, at the time of making any or final payment by his Affidavit, by Certificate from Clerk of Record Office or by liens, releases or other legal proof, that the property is free from all liens or claims against the premises or the said Contractor....for work or materials furnished on said works.

AND IT IS HEREBY FURTHER AGREED, BY AND BETWEEN THE SAID PARTIES:

first.—That the Specifications and Drawings are intended to co-operate, so that any works exhibited in the Drawings, and not mentioned in the Specifications, or vice-versa, are to be executed the same as if mentioned in the Specification and set forth in the Drawings, to the true intent and meaning of the said Drawings and Specifications.

Second.—The Contractor, at his.......own proper cost and charges, is ....to provide all manner of labor materials, apparatus, scaffolding, utensils and cartage, of every description, needful for the due performance of the several works; must produce, whenever required by Superintendent or Proprietor...., all vouchers showing the quality of goods and materials used; and render all due and sufficient facilities to the Architect.., Superintendent or Clerk of Works, for the proper inspection of the works and materials, and which are to be under their control; and they may require the Contractor to dismiss any workman or workmen who they may think incompetent or improper to be employed; the workmen and Contractor being only admitted to the ground for the purpose of the proper execution of the works, and have no tenancy. The Contractor..shall deliver up the works to the Proprietor.. in perfect repair, clean and in good condition, when complete. The Contractor..shall not sub-let the works, or any part thereof, without consent in writing of the Proprietor.. or Architect..

Third.—Should the Proprietor..at any time during the progress of the said works, require any alterations of, deviations from, additions to, or omissions in the said Contract, Specifications or Plans, he........shall have the right and power to make such change or changes, and the same shall in no way injuriously affect or make void the Contract; but the difference for work omitted, shall be deducted from the amount of the Contract, by a fair and reasonable valuation; and for additional work required in alterations, the amount based upon same prices at which contract is taken shall be agreed upon before commencing additions, as provided and hereinafter set forth in Article No. 6; and such agreement shall state also the extension of time (if any) which is to be granted by reason thereof.

fourth.—Should the Contractor.., at any time during the progress of said works, become bankrupt, refuse or neglect to supply a sufficiency of material or of workmen, or cause any unreasonable neglect or suspension of work, or fail or refuse to follow the Drawings and Specifications, or comply with any of the Articles of Agreement, the Proprietor..or his...... Agent, shall have the right and power to enter upon and take possession of the premises, and may at once terminate the Contract, whereupon all claim of the Contractor.., his....executors administrators or assigns, shall cease; and the Proprietor..may provide materials and workmen sufficient to complete the said works, after giving forty-eight hours notice, in writing, directed and delivered to the Contractor.. or at his......residence or place of business; and the expense of the notice and the completing of the various works will be deducted from the amount of the Contract, or any part of it due, or to become due, to the Contractor..; and in such case no scaffolding or fixed tackle of any kind, belonging to such Contractor.., shall be removed, so long as the same is wanted for the work.... But if any balance on the amount of this Contract remains after completion in respect of work done during the time of the defaulting Contractor.., the same shall belong to the persons legally representing him.... but the Proprietor..shall not be liable or accountable to them in any way for the manner in which he.. may have gotten the work completed.

fifth.—Should any dispute arise respecting the true construction or meaning of the Drawings or Specifications, as to what is extra work outside of Contract, the same shall be decided by....F. J. Camp....Architect.., and his......decision shall be final and conclusive; or in the event of his......death or unwillingness to act, then of some other known capable Architect, Competent Clerk of Works or Foreman, to be appointed by the Proprietor..; but should any dispute arise respecting the true value of any....work....omitted by the Contractor.., the same shall be valued by two competent persons, one employed by the Proprietor.., and the other by the Contractor.., and these two shall have power to name an umpire, whose decision shall be binding on all parties.

Sixth.—No new work or any description done on the premises, or any work of any kind whatsoever shall be considered as extra unless a separate estimate in writing for the same, before its commencement, shall have been submitted by the Contractor..to the Superintendent and the Proprietor.., and their signatures obtained thereto, and the Contractor..shall demand payment for such work immediately it is done. In case of day's work, statement of the same must be delivered to the Proprietor at latest during the week following that in which the work may have been done, and only such day's work and extra work will be paid for, as such, as agreed on and authorized in writing.

Seventh.—The Proprietor..will not, in any manner, be answerable or accountable for any loss or damage that shall or may happen to the said works, or any part or parts thereof respectively or for any of the materials or other things used and employed in finishing and completing the said works; or for injury to any person or persons, either workmen or the public, or for damage to adjoining property, from any cause which might have been prevented by the Contractor.., his......workmen, or any one employed by him......against all which injuries and damages to persons and property, the Contractor..having control over such work must properly guard against, and must make good all damage from whatever cause, being strictly responsible for the same. Where there are different Contractors employed on the works, each shall be responsible to the other for all damage to work, to persons or property, or for loss caused by neglect, by failure to finish work at proper time and preventing each portion of the works being finished by the several Contractors at date mentioned in this Contract for completion, or from any other cause; and any Contractor suffering damage shall call the attention of the Proprietor..or Superintendent..to the same, for action as laid down in Article No. 4.

Eighth.—The Owner will insure the building......in the joint names and interest of himself and the Contractor..against loss or damage by fire in such sums as may from time to time be agreed on with the Contractor..to cover work and materials used in the building and around the premises, and the policies to be made payable to owner and contractor..as their interest may appear. The Contractor..shall see to it that this insurance is effected to his full satisfaction, and the cost of same will be borne by the Contractor..and for any loss of the Contractor.. by fire, the owner will not, under any circumstances, be answerable or accountable.

Ninth.—All work and materials, as delivered on the premises to form part of the works, are to be considered the property of the Proprietor.., and are not to be removed without his......consent; but the Contractor..shall have the right to remove all surplus materials after his......completing the works.

Tenth.—Should the Contractor..fail to finish the work at or before the time agreed upon........shall pay to, or allow the Proprietor.., by way of liquidated damages, the sum of........ dollars per diem, for each and every day thereafter the said works remain incomplete.

Eleventh.—

In Witness Whereof, the said parties have hereunto set their names and seals the day and year above written.

Signed, sealed and delivered in the presence of

Witness:_____   Part of the First Part:_____

Witness:_____   Part of the Second Part: O. H. Yates   Prest:

SPECIFICATION

--of the--

Labor and Materials required in the Plumbing of the Auditorium Building, for the Ocean Grove Camp Meeting Association, at Ocean Grove, N. J. from plans by F. T. CAMP, Architect, No. 114 Nassau Street, N. Y. City.

--00O00--

Conditions:-

These plans and specifications are intended to so co-operate, that a complete job of plumbing is to be done, according to the intent and meaning of these presents, and everything requisite to the entire completion of the plumbing, as herein shown, is to be furnished and done, whether each item be mentioned or drawn or not, and no extras of any kind will be allowed unless the same is in addition to the work herein described, and is authorized by the Architect in writing, as directed by the Building Committee.

Water Closets to be the best pattern of "wash outs" with wooden seat and lid, secured to the bowl, and supplied with cold water through 1 1/4 D lead pipe from iron cisterns which are supplied by 1/2" A lead pipe from main.

Service pipe from street to be 1" galvanized iron, with stop cock inside cellar wall. Urinal of corner pattern lipped, and supplied with water through 1/2" A lead pipe, and N. P. faucet, and wasted through 1 1/2" D lead pipe and trap, and connected to soil pipe outside of closet trap, and trap ventilated by the McClellan trap vent. W.C. trap connected by ventilation pipe to the same trap vent.

Wash basin of marbled porcelain, set in 1 1/4" marble slab, molded and countersunk, and 1" marble molded

J. S. Flitcroft + Bro.

IMPROVED
Agreement for Building.
WITH BOND.

BETWEEN

J. S. Flitcroft + Bro
Plumber

OF THE FIRST PART,

—AND—

Ocean Grove Camp
Meeting Association

OF THE SECOND PART,

Dated *Dec. 12th* 1893

Filed _____ 189_

ARCHITECT
F. T. Camp
114. Nassau St. N.Y.

PALLISER, PALLISER & CO.,
Publishers Fine Architectural Works,
24 E. 2nd St., NEW YORK CITY.

Price each, 5 Cents; per dozen, 40 Cents; 40 for $1.00;
100 for $2.00.

BOND.

Know all Men by these Presents. That I, *John S. Flitcroft*

backs, and supplied with water through 1/2" A lead pipe and N. P. faucet, - low and short spout, and plated chain, plug, and chain stay.

Wasted through 1 1/2" D lead pipe and trap, and trap ventilated by the McClellan trap vent, making one trap vent for each set of fixtures.

Water Closets will be set on a stove board, which will be treated like a marble slab, and no other woodwork, than seat and lid, will be around closets. Basin will be supported by a neat pattern of fancy bronzed brackets, screwed to wooden cleats, screwed to wall by Carpenter.

Water and pipes from the Association's mains will be brought into cellar by the Association, and stop cocks ap- plied by this contractor.

Water will be brought into boiler room through a 2" galvanized iron main, with a stop cock at cellar walls and a 3" blow off outlet will be put in and connected to outlet for this purpose provided by mason.

Bidders must state in their bids the number of working days they will require to execute the work in this contract.

Wiring and Fixtures Contract

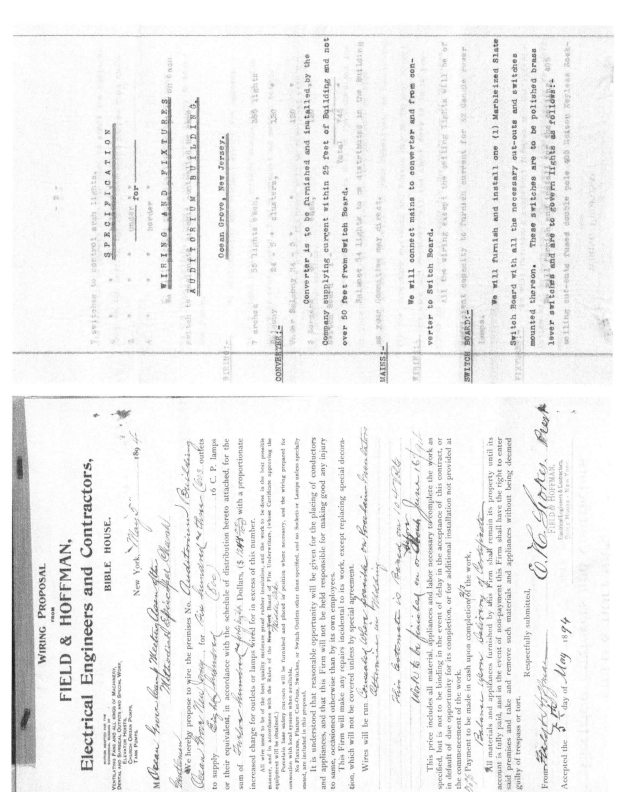

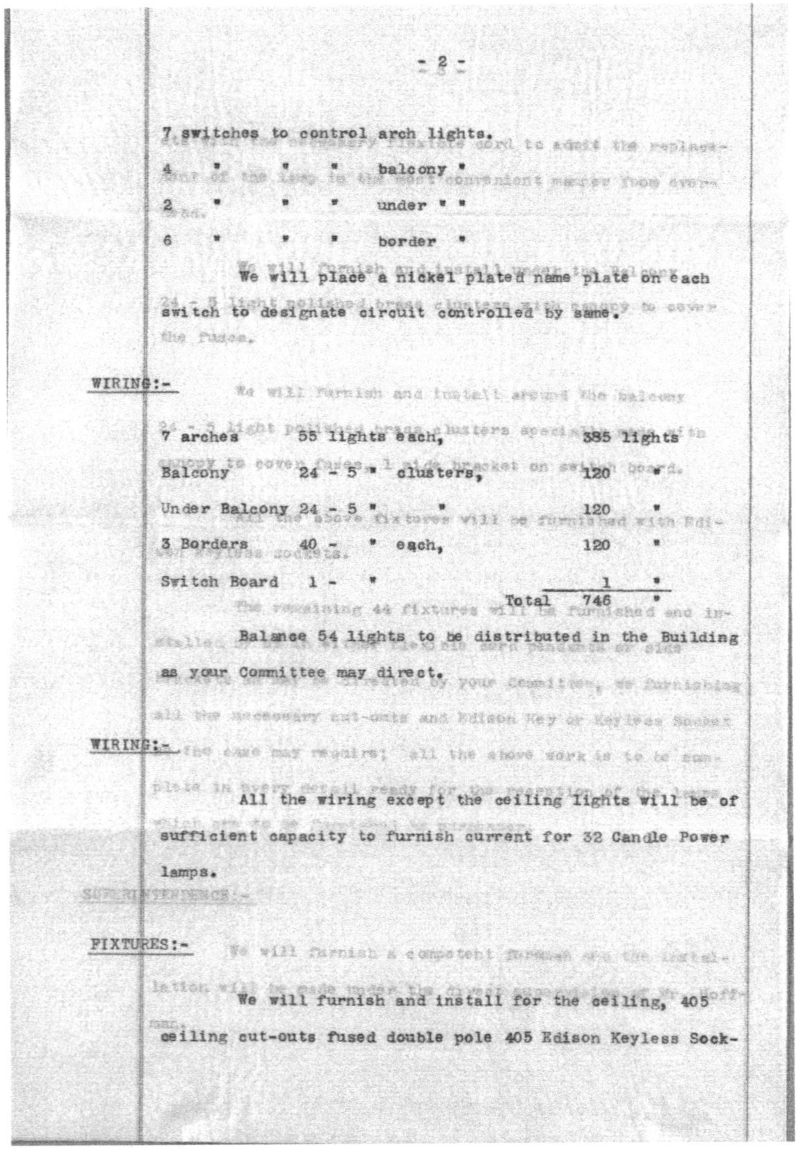

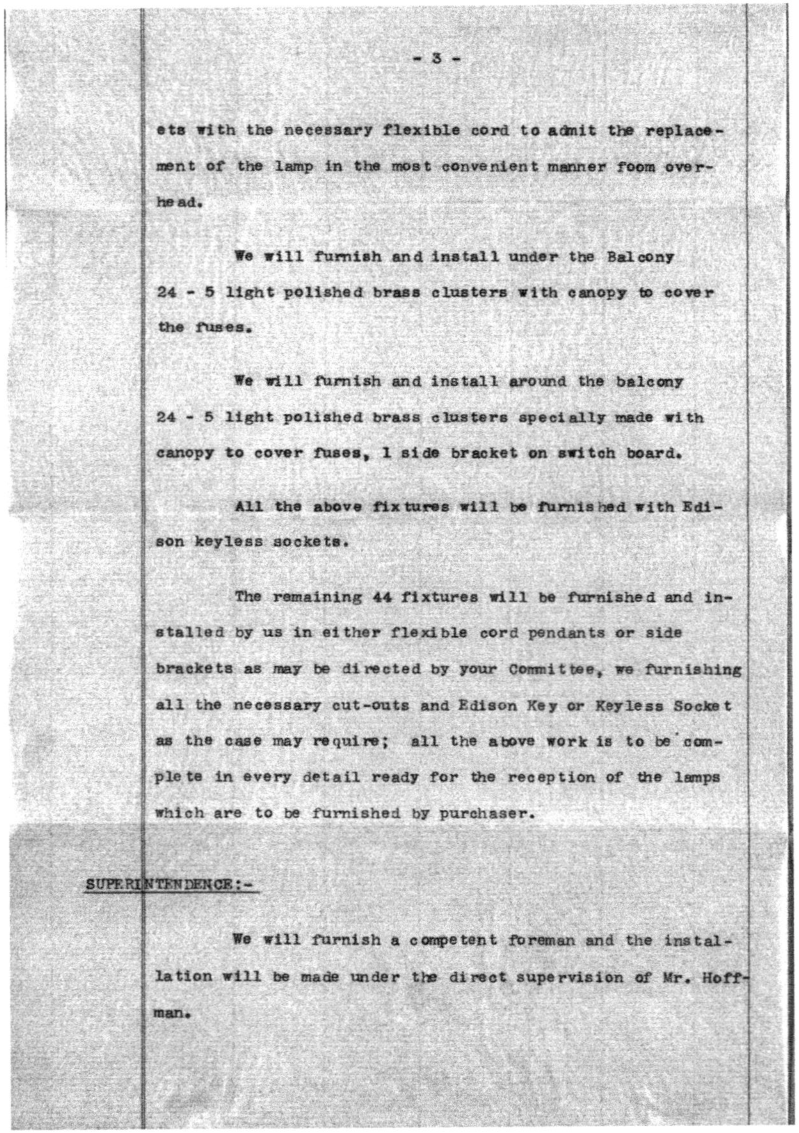

- 3 -

ets with the necessary flexible cord to admit the replacement of the lamp in the most convenient manner from overhead.

We will furnish and install under the Balcony
24 - 5 light polished brass clusters with canopy to cover
the fuses.

We will furnish and install around the balcony
24 - 5 light polished brass clusters specially made with
canopy to cover fuses, 1 side bracket on switch board.

All the above fixtures will be furnished with Edison keyless sockets.

The remaining 44 fixtures will be furnished and installed by us in either flexible cord pendants or side
brackets as may be directed by your Committee, we furnishing
all the necessary cut-outs and Edison Key or Keyless Socket
as the case may require; all the above work is to be complete in every detail ready for the reception of the lamps
which are to be furnished by purchaser.

SUPERINTENDENCE:-

We will furnish a competent foreman and the installation will be made under the direct supervision of Mr. Hoffman.

- 2 -

7 switches to control arch lights.
4 " " " balcony.
2 " " " under " "
6 " " " border "

We will place a nickel plated name plate on each
24 - 5 light switch to designate circuit controlled by same, to cover
the fuses.

WIRING:-
We will furnish and install around the balcony

7 arches 55 lights each, clusters approx 385 lights in
Balcony 24 - 5 " clusters, on 120 board
Under Balcony 24 - 5 " " fixtures will be furnished with Edi- 120 "
3 Borders 40 - " each, 120 "
Switch Board 1 - " 1 "
                         Total 746 "

The remaining 44 fixtures will be furnished and in-
Balance 54 lights to be distributed in the Building
as may be directed by your Committee, we furnishing
as your Committee may direct.

all the necessary cut-outs and Edison Key or Keyless Socket
WIRING:- the case may require; all the above work is to be complete in

All the wiring except the ceiling lights will be of
sufficient capacity to furnish current for 32 Candle Power
lamps.

FIXTURES:-
We will furnish a competent foreman and the installation will be made under the direct supervision of Mr. Hoff-
We will furnish and install for the ceiling, 405
ceiling cut-outs fused double pole 405 Edison Keyless Sock-

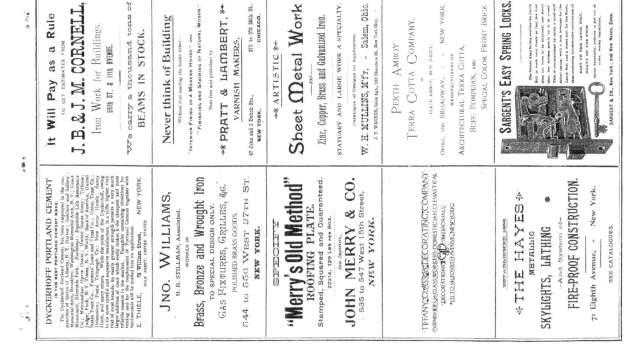

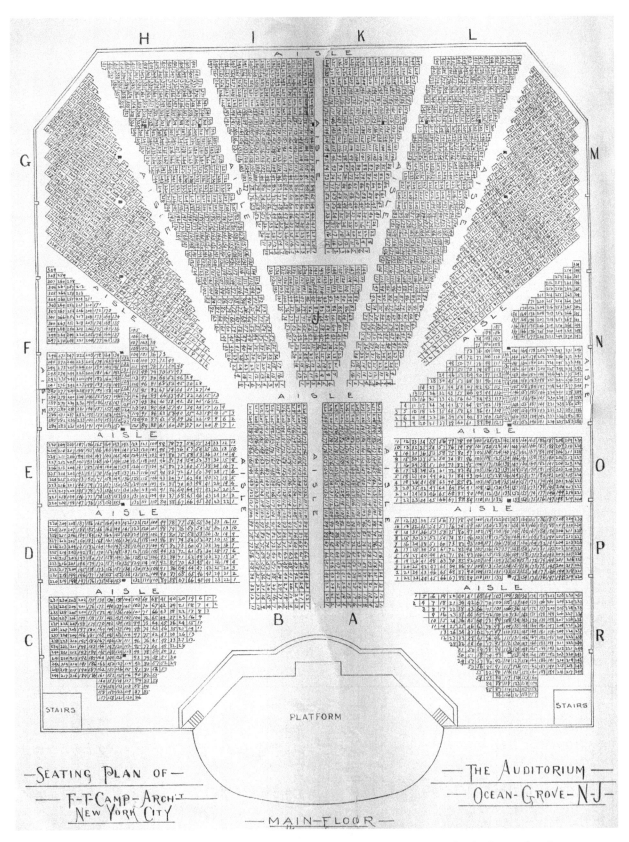

The main floor seating plan for 4,750 seats by Fred. T. Camp, architect, with each seat individually numbered.

Chapter Seven

AUDITORIUM SEATS

For the first twenty-five years of worship services, Ocean Grove congregants sat clustered on park-like benches, scattered among the trees in Auditorium Square. Several early photos clearly show these slat-back benches on the dirt ground. The Camp Meeting had purchased one group of cast-iron frame settees from the Pitman (NJ) Camp Meeting, and utilized them for many summer seasons.

The new Auditorium with its sloping wood floor and sprawling ceiling would certainly require a much better quality seat for the worshippers sitting for hours listening to speakers. "The present Auditorium seats are hard and wearisome for long sittings," reports the *Ocean Grove Record* on August 5, 1893. "We need something better. The Auditorium will be seated with chairs

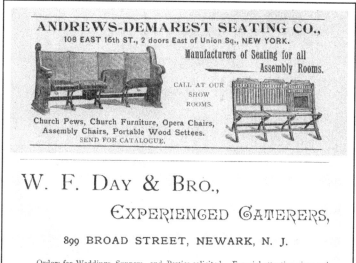

An advertisement by the Andrews-Demarest Seating Company in the 1894 Newark Conference Report. The company was a major supplier of church pews and assembly chairs. Also advertised was an ad by W.F. Day and Bro. for ice cream in Ocean Grove. Day's is a favorite location for an ice cream treat after the weekly services.

of modern pattern, affording comfort instead of pain. All hail the chairs!" And like other public meeting houses constructed during this time, individual seating was preferred over bench seating.

The Camp Meeting ordered 6,000 individual chairs for the new Auditorium from the Andrews-Demarest Seating Co., located at 108 East 16th Street, New York City, NY. The memorandum of agreement was signed on December 30, 1893, with delivery on or before June 20, 1894. The price of these chairs was 60 cents each, for a total of $3,600.

The chairs were described as No. 70 special folding seat chairs or settees, "all to be made with Catskill Mountain rock maple frame, finished in the natural color of the wood, with curved back with spindles and curved framed seat covered with a red fiber seating. The foot rail is to have rounded top edge and rail on rear of seat, to be beveled on the inside edge. All seating to be nineteen (19) inches wide to centers and made to fit." The original seating plan was prepared by Frederick Camp, as the diagrams demonstrate.

One term of the contract provided free delivery of the 6,000 chairs to the Ocean Grove Railroad Station. This initial order also purchased 6,000 hat racks with necessary screw eyes to be fastened

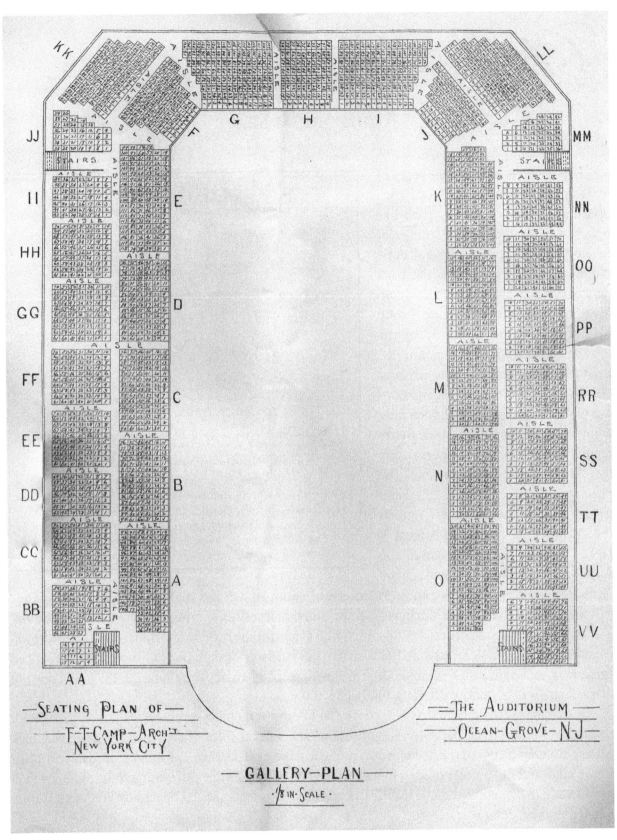

The gallery plan for 2,653 seats. There are only four exits from the gallery, in Sections AA, JJ, MM, and VV.

❧ Wayne T. Bell, Jr. ❧ Cindy L. Bell ❧ Darrell A. Dufresne❧

by Camp Meeting workers to the bottom frame of the new seats. On a warm Tuesday in June 1893, ten heavily laden railroad cars pulled up to the freight station to unload the 6,000 wooden folding chairs, pre-numbered and joined in sets of three, four and five.

The OGCMA salvaged the iron frame settees from the previous Auditorium for installation in the upper tier galleries of the new building; this provided seating for approximately 3,600 persons. One stipulation in this contract provided the OGCMA with a two-year window to purchase an additional 4,000 chairs at 60 cents each if they decided to replace these old iron 1874 frame settees. Another provision involved the free replacement of any fiber seats which may prove defective in actual use during the 1894 Camp Meeting season. The company would supply two additional fiber seats for any defective seat. This specific Agreement illustrates how cost-conscious the OGCMA was in its construction and furnishing of the Auditorium.

In spring 1897, the Andrews-Demarest Company encountered business troubles caused by a slow down in orders for opera houses, public buildings and church furniture and in the collection of monies owed from various clients. Perhaps if the OGCMA had ordered those extra 4,000 maple chairs, the company would be in business today. But congregants were apparently willing to squeeze onto those balcony settees, making room for one more visitor to the Auditorium.

"So how many seats are in the Great Auditorium?" is a question frequently asked by those strolling past the building. Early postcard views of the interior of the Auditorium sport catchy phrases of "Seating capacity of nearly 10,000." Clearly, the Request for Proposals and the subsequent Memorandum of Agreement are the probable sources of this seating number of 10,000 (6,000 chairs plus 4,000 additional chairs from the contract terms). However, this number was adjusted to 9,600 in the 1894 Annual Report, with a count of 5,244 folding chairs on the lower floor, 355 in the platform/choir area and approximately 3,600 settee seats in the gallery, for a total of 9,600 seats. Interestingly enough, Camp's original seating diagram for the Auditorium was for 7,758 seats: 4,750 seats on the main floor, 2,653 seats in the gallery, and 355 platform/choir seats.

A reduction of gallery seats occurred in 1907-1908 when two new gallery exits were added at the midpoint of the south and north sides of the Auditorium (Sections FF and RR). These exits have

The underside of the southeast staircase once functioned as a ticket booth.

a partially covered roof and extend directly out from the building. This was not always the case as one photo shows a staircase filled with children running adjacent to the northwest MM Section.

The Auditorium balcony (referred to by ushers as the gallery) is often the recipient of used seating. In the late 1950s, when the Strand Theatre at the North End upgraded the movie theater, their Art Deco style chairs featuring solid wood backs and cast iron arm rests were installed in the Auditorium balcony, replacing many of the 1874 iron-framed settees. Then, in 1961, new theatre-style cushioned seats were installed in the Auditorium's main lower level sections. An order was placed with the Irwin Seating Company of Grand Rapids, Michigan, for 1,044 light green upholstered seats with salmon-colored arms. On the back of most of these chairs is a small

This early photo of music director Tali Esen Morgan and Ocean Grove youngsters shows the northwest gallery stairs running adjacent to the building. These stairs were repositioned 45 degrees to run straight out from the building, probably when additional gallery stairs were added in 1908.

Art Deco style seats from the North End Strand Theater. Most of these seats have wire hat racks.

dedication plaque, as Camp Meeting supporters purchased chairs in memory of loved ones. Other dedicated seats have been added until about 80% of the main floor is theatre style cushioned seats.

Once again, the balcony was the recipient of the main floor's 65-year old maple chairs, as the last of the 1874 settees were removed. This significant change in the main floor seating and aisle layout reduced the total number to approximately 6,700 seats. For instance, in 1894, Floor Sections A and B had eleven seats per row with the pre-fabricated chair sets of 4/4/3 or 5/3/3. To accommodate the current seating plan of 12 seats across in Sections A and B, the sections were expanded outward.

The main floor wooden chairs were moved to the balcony to replace the Pitman Grove camp meeting settees. The one challenge was that most of these chairs had their two back legs shortened to conform to the slope of the main floor. This problem was solved by Trustee Jack Green, Operations Chairman of the OGCMA, by the placement of a wooden strip on the floor at the back of the seat rows in the balcony. The chairs were then at an upright level position.

From the 1920s through the 1940s, two Auditorium seats could be reserved for a small fee. The ever-friendly Ocean Grove Usher assigned to your seating section would unlock a small padlock attached to the bottom of the seat by a hasp and a screw eye, making the two seats available for use. Most of the hasps have been removed but you can still find one or two of the Andrew-Demarest seats with the hasp and hat rack attached under the seat. The photo from the late 1950s clearly shows the mixture of three different styles of seats found in the balcony at one time: the iron frame settees (to the right) purchased from Pitman Grove; the Andrews-Demarest maple chairs (front three rows of the balcony and the main floor),

A row of Andrews-Demarest chairs, originally located on the sloping main floor, are leveled in the balcony by placing a strip of wood under the rear legs.

An example of a 'reserved seat' lock.

and the Art Deco theater seats (lower right corner of photo) from the Strand Theater. Mr. Joseph Thoma, former executive director of the OGCMA, is shown looking over the main floor. This photo is taken before the present theater-style seats were installed in 1961. Other points of interest in the photo include the small cross above the flag, the large cross to the left and the crown to the right. Notice that the main entrance to the choir loft is in the center with the pulpit at the center of the platform. Behind the altar rail is a double line of chairs. In the middle is the white marble Baptismal Font, a gift of Mrs. Ellen Vernor Simpson, the wife of Bishop Mathew Simpson. The Font has been relocated to the Bishop Janes Tabernacle as has the Pulpit with the onyx slab.

The most recent changes in Auditorium seating resulted from the 2008 installation of the Echo Gallery Organ, constructed by A.R. Schopp's Sons of Alliance, Ohio, which reduced the balcony seating somewhat. In addition, some seats on the lower level were removed to accommodate wheel chair seating and sound equipment. The exact number of seats in the Auditorium as of the date of this book is 6,662. However, during guided tours of the Auditorium, it is just easier to claim seating for 6,700, give or take a few.

Finally, the theatre seats behind the organ were replaced in 1999 with wooden, padded pews, whose graceful arc reflects the architectural

Three types of seats in the Auditorium are shown in this photograph.

design of the parabolic ceiling. This enhancement was made possible by a $60,000 donation from the Ocean Grove Refreshment Staff, a group of volunteers who raised the funds by selling soda and hot dogs at the Saturday night programs.

In 1999, cushioned pews replaced the theater seats in the choir loft.

(right) A current photo of the Great Auditorium filled with worshippers on Choir Festival Sunday, taken by Stephen Hirt from the choir loft.

(below) An annual photo of the Auditorium Ushers, who put in uncounted hours for special programs, Saturday night concerts and Sunday services. The precision of the ushers' corps, in their blue blazers and white trousers, collecting the weekly offering is a special happening, not to be missed. Photo courtesy of RJB Photographers.

Auditorium Seats Contract

MEMORANDUM OF AGREEMENT made this 30th day of December, 1893

between

Andrews-Demarest Seating Co., 106 East 16th St., New York City, N. Y.

first party

and

The Ocean Grove Camp Meeting Association of the Methodist Episcopal Church, Ocean Grove, in the County of Monmouth, State of New Jersey.

second party.

1st: The first party agrees to make for the second party, the number and style of chairs set forth in the following schedule and deliver the same free on board the cars at Ocean Grove Railroad Station at Ocean Grove, New Jersey, on or before the 20th day of June, 1894.

About six thousand (6,000) No. 70 special folding seat chairs or settees, per sample shown; all to be made with Catskill Mountain rock maple frame, finished the natural color of the wood, with curved back with spindles and with curved framed seat covered with red fibre seating. Foot rail to have round-ed top edge and rail or rear of seat to be beveled on the inside edge. All seating to be nineteen (19) inches wide to centres and made to fit plan to be adopted according to sections four, five, six and seven. First party to furnish free of charge, hat racks for all sittings with necessary screw eyes fastened in the frame of settees to receive said racks. The racks to be put in place by party of the second part. The first party further agrees to send without charge to second party, workmen to Ocean Grove previous to opening of season of 1895 and replace all fibre seats which may have proved defective in actual use and furnish two additional

fibre seats for each one of said defective seats, if any.

2nd: The price of the said chairs or settees is as follows:- No. 70 Special -- One 60/100 Dollars per sitting.

3rd: The price thereof is to be paid as follows: the net amount of bill to be paid in cash upon satisfactory completion of contract by party of first part, in accordance with terms of supplementary contract.

4th: The second party shall furnish within twelve (12) days from the date hereof a complete plan, drawn to scale, giving exact outlines of auditorium where seats are to be placed, also exact location of aisles, platforms, posts, heaters, registers, doors and other obstructions &c. The plan shall accurately show width of steps, height of risers, or slope of floor and all other details necessary to enable the first party to perform their part of this contract.

5th: From said plan the first party will make a complete seating plan, showing number and arrangement of seating, with number of seats in each section which shall be submitted to the second party or their agent on or before January 15th for their approval. This submitted plan shall be approved or disapproved before January 20th and if disapproved the second party or their agent must notify the first party in writing before January 21st of the changes to be made in said plan and when such changes are made in accordance with the directions of the second party or their agent, the said plan shall then be deemed approved and when so approved, the number of seats shown thereon shall be the number ordered and accepted by second party.

6th: The first party shall not be held accountable for any errors of measurements in plan of house or of any alterations or changes in building the house after plan is approved and

3374

Andrus, Demarest, Seating Co
&
The Ocean Grove Camp Meeting
Association of the M.E. Church.

Filed January 19, 1894
Theo Cammack
Clk

5.

accepted by second party or their agent.

7th: It is further agreed that should the second party, or their
agent fail to furnish the plans, within the time fixed, then
for each day's delay the first party shall be allowed one day
additional in the sets to be performed by them.

8th: Any difference arising between the parties to the foregoing agreement as to its meaning or fulfillment shall be
submitted to the arbitration and award of arbitrators, mutually chosen, and failing to agree upon arbitrators, each party
shall name one and the two thus chosen shall choose a third
and the decision and award of any two of them shall be binding
upon the parties hereto.

9th: It is further agreed that first party shall furnish to second
party about four thousand (4,000) additional folding seat
chairs or settees of the same style as above mentioned and
on the same terms if said second party shall decide to replace
the iron frame settees they now have for gallery of the new
Auditorium within two years from the date of this contract.
The same time to be allowed party of the first part for the
manufacture of said four thousand (4,000) sittings as allowed
for the manufacture of the six thousand (6,000) sittings for
present delivery and the entire four thousand (4,000) sittings
to be included in one order. The exact number of additional
seats to be determined by seating plan &c. as in present order.

Andrus Demarest Seating Co.
E. H. Stokes, Prest
O.G.C.M. Association

Chapter Eight

THE SCIENCE OF SOUND AND OTHER ACOUSTICAL PROPERTIES

A very true friend, looking at the vast proportions of the new Auditorium, wrote to President Stokes, "Where will you find a man with voice loud enough and strong enough to fill it?" The reply was, "Even a whisper can be distinctly heard in the remotest part of the room." The design of the hanging wooden parabolic ceiling is one of the most important factors in the success of the Auditorium. The Auditorium would have been a failure if the assembled worshipers could not hear the preachers or choirs. Architect Fred Camp discussed the sound issue in an interview with a reporter from the *New York Daily Tribune* on February 19, 1894.

"The acoustic properties," said the architect, F.T. Camp, "have been carefully figured out and fully 90 per cent of the largest audience will find no difficulty in hearing every word. The lines of the ceiling are parabolic from front to rear and from side to side, while the ends are polygonal, and in addition there is to be at rear of platform a parabolic sounding board attached to the vertical walls, and over the speaker there will be a smaller section of sounding-board, with the same parabolic outline. All these precautions will result in the waves of the voice being sent forward and outward in such a shape that by no possibility can echoes be produced."

A children's choir directed by Tali Esen Morgan waits to sing under the curved parabolic shell. The pipes behind the choir are from the first organ; this photo is before 1907.

"But the scheme also embraces as a strong factor, the use of a system of forced ventilation to aid the effectual dissemination of the voice, by inducing a gentle current outward and downward from the speaker, and this result is attained by withdrawing or exhausting from the floor, along the centre and well toward the rear, through registers or gratings and large ducts, a volume of air of about 5,000 cubic feet every minute, and by the use of fans, throwing it up through the two front turrets above the roofs," Camp explained. (See Chapter 9 on Ventilation for discussion of this issue.)

So impressive were the natural acoustics of the Auditorium that a reporter's interview and personal tour of the facility with Dr. Stokes resulted in the following article in the 1894 *Ocean Grove Record*:

The Science of Sound

As we approach the supreme hour which shall determine success or failure of the new Ocean Grove Auditorium in regards to its acoustical properties, the interest in this question has become intense. Until within a few days the interior of the mammoth edifice has been in no favorable condition to make tests that proved entirely satisfactory; although the indications all pointed to a result which should answer, and more than meet every reasonable expectation.

At the twilight hour of Wednesday last, Dr. Stokes, who had been spending the evening in company with other friends with the family of Rev. S. H. Asay at the Holland House, was called out to gratify the curiosity of some visitors on the grounds in regards to this very matter. The ceiling had been completed, the platform erected and the flooring partly laid. It was a quiet and suitable hour to try the human voice and discover if such a nuisance as an echo existed, and its cause and remedy.

The Doctor invited any who wished to do so to accompany him, and seeing a dozen or so entering the building, twice the number of loiterers around availed themselves of the privilege they never had offered them before, and were admitted. The company on the spacious floor was requested to retire to the remotest point on and under the western end gallery. Dr. Stokes stood on the platform, and beside him stood Rev. H. C. Mead, of the Silver Lake Quartet. These two conversed in ordinary tones and the people away under the galleries heard every word. The Doctor then repeated the Lord's Prayer in subdued voice, and not a syllable was lost in any part of the building. He then uttered a sentence oratorically, repeated it in lower and still lower tones until he actually came to a whisper, and even the whisper was heard with startling distinctiveness by persons far removed from where he stood.

Rev. Bro. Mead was asked to sing, and his one stanza "The Child of a King" filled the concave with melody. Efforts were made to produce an echo, but while the resonance was pleasing we detected nothing defective in a distinct voice. True, every voice is not like that of Dr. Stokes or H. C. Mead. But if speakers can only remain as self-possessed as the Doctor, and not talk too loud, we expect the acoustics as wonderfully agreeable as the building itself will be adjudged a model of symmetry, and architectural expansiveness and beauty.

One more experiment was made on Wednesday evening which we consider extraordinary. Dr. Stokes took out his pocket knife and called for silences, opened and shut the blade with a little click, and this also was heard some distance from the platform. It is said of the Mormon Temple at Salt Lake, that one could hear a pin drop. This may be only hyperbole, but for an audience literally, and all its purposes, the highest hopes are entertained that our new building will prove a delight to both speakers and hearers during the present and coming years.

(above) Another early photo of the front of the Auditorium. Light streams in the upper windows, which are now blocked by ranks of organ pipes. The center entrance under the choir loft was closed with modernizations.

(right) A three dimensional drawing of the relationship of the organ pipe chambers, courtesy of David Fox.

Author Darrell Dufresne standing at the top of the choir loft next to a rank of 16-foot pedal diapason pipes. Once decorative, this set of pipes is now in full voice.

Specifications in the Carpentry Contract list two sounding boards to be constructed at the east and west ends of the building. The west board was never constructed. A picture of the east parabolic sounding board shows the structure behind the pipes of the Washington Square organ donated in 1895. Much of the sounding board was removed during the installation of the Hope-Jones organ and the subsequent eastward expansion of the front of the Auditorium in 1907-1908. The top part of the parabolic curve can still be seen above the current rank of pipes.

A description of The Storm, an original organ composition that illustrates the versatility of the Hope-Jones organ.

The present organ console, originally built by the Aeolian Company, is the fifth to control the organ. It was installed in 1986 and boasts five manuals, 176 ranks and 10,823 pipes.

Over the years several sound studies have examined the acoustics of the Auditorium. Tests conducted in 2003 by an architectural acoustic firm "confirm that the Great Auditorium has a very unique acoustic signature. The best seats in the house for viewing are not the best seats for listening and vice versa." Even professional singers are impressed with the natural resonance of the Auditorium. Many locals will recall the hot summer night in 1992 when singer Tony Bennett suggested the sound system be turned off, and he stood at the front edge of the stage, before a crowd of some 5,000, singing a cappella. He was heard by everyone. He repeated this in his 2011 performance, proving that the Auditorium continues to delight speakers and listeners in the twenty-first century.

The organ console and the center stairway are located behind the five soloists and conductor. Some 190 people participated in the St. Paul's Day Festival of Haydn's Creation in 1947, directed by Thelma Mount (second from right). The choir is seated on the 1894 Andrews-Demarest chairs.

Chapter Nine

Ventilation: Mystery and Myth

Victorians were concerned with moving air to keep cool and to promote good health. The prevalent thinking in Victorian times was that still air was impure and promoted growth of diseases and molds. Health could only be assured if houses and public spaces were well-ventilated. Initially, this problem of stagnant air was resolved by the use of natural ventilation concepts with the development of stacks, chimneys and door transoms within a building and a thorough knowledge of surrounding wind and temperature patterns. Even today, many working farm barns rely on natural ventilation to exchange air around livestock. This simple system of natural ventilation was soon replaced by mechanical means of sheet metal ducts and fans either pulling or pushing air through buildings. In some "modern" 1890 buildings the air entering a building was cooled by passage over

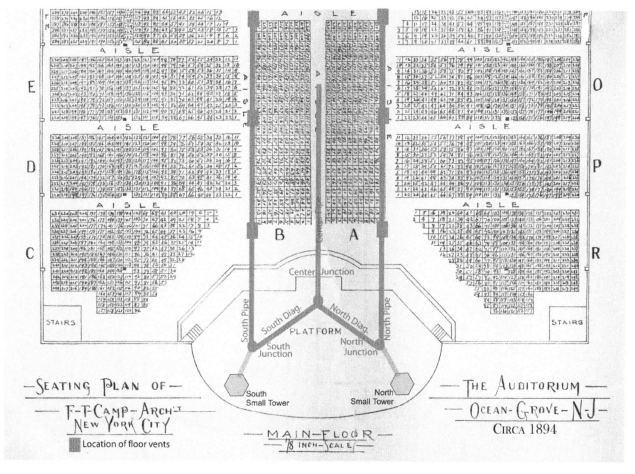

This is architect Fred Camp's seating plan for the Auditorium in 1894, amended to show the locations of the six floor grates on the north and south wooden pipes. Note how the outer pipes run to the bottom of the two small towers and also connect to the center pipe under the stage. There is no evidence of the center pipe having floor vents or a fan.

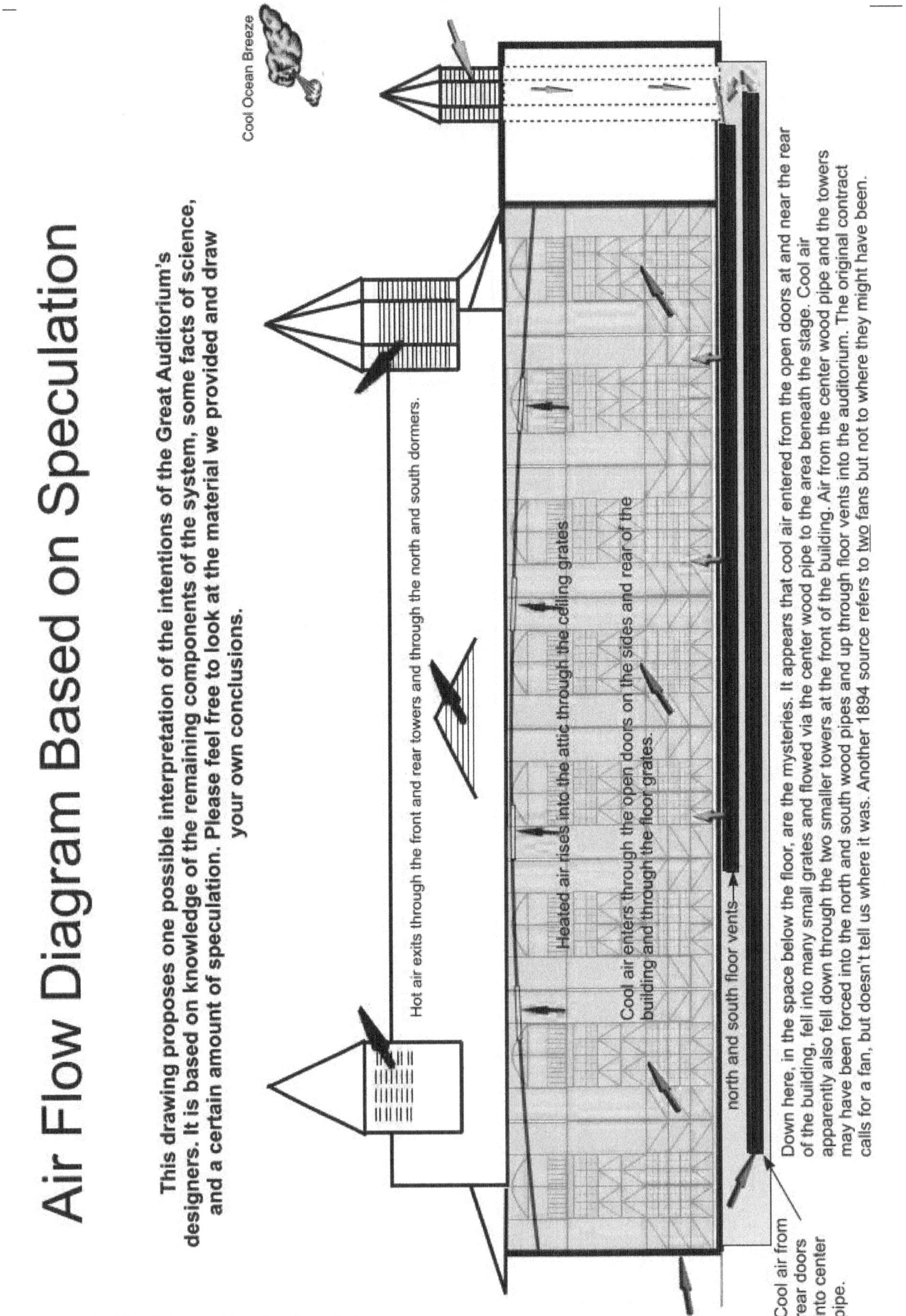

Air Flow Diagram Based on Speculation

This drawing proposes one possible interpretation of the intentions of the Great Auditorium's designers. It is based on knowledge of the remaining components of the system, some facts of science, and a certain amount of speculation. Please feel free to look at the material we provided and draw your own conclusions.

Cool Ocean Breeze

Hot air exits through the front and rear towers and through the north and south dormers.

Heated air rises into the attic through the ceiling grates

Cool air enters through the open doors on the sides and rear of the building and through the floor grates.

north and south floor vents

Cool air from rear doors into center pipe.

Down here, in the space below the floor, are the mysteries. It appears that cool air entered from the open doors at and near the rear of the building, fell into many small grates and flowed via the center wood pipe to the area beneath the stage. Cool air apparently also fell down through the two smaller towers at the front of the building. Air from the center wood pipe and the towers may have been forced into the north and south wood pipes and up through floor vents into the auditorium. The original contract calls for a fan, but doesn't tell us where it was. Another 1894 source refers to two fans but not to where they might have been.

Air Flow Diagram Based on Speculation.

blocks of ice - the early beginnings of air conditioning, as exemplified by the Roosevelt University Auditorium Theatre in Chicago.

The "Doctor Breeze" is a well known phenomenon along seashores and large lakes. Movement of air is based on the temperature difference between the land and water. On a summer day in the morning, the breeze is typically from the land to the water. In the afternoon, the breeze is usually from the water toward the land, the land now being warmer than the water. The setback design by Ocean Grove's founder William Osborn channels the sea/land breeze via the 1,500 foot Ocean Pathway (and other east-west avenues) illustrating a remarkable vision in urban planning: natural air conditioning.

Myth

Obviously, the design of a building with seating capacity for nearly 10,000 must consider air flow, but first, there is a longtime myth told around Ocean Grove. There is a persistent story about big wooden pipes running under the ground of Ocean Pathway from the beach to the Auditorium, carrying refreshing ocean air under the floor of the Auditorium to cool the worshipers. If this were true, it would be fascinating to dig it up and learn how it was built. But this is a myth – there are no big wooden ventilation pipes under Ocean Pathway. Not only is there no record of such a system, if could work only if the wind direction was always due west. A very large structure would need to catch and channel the air into the pipes and eventually, sand would be carried in and block the pipes. There are no pipes from the beach, but there are pipes under the Auditorium floor.

Camp's Ventilation Plan

There are several references about pipes and the air exchange ventilation design of the Auditorium: two are found in the 1894 Annual Report of the Camp Meeting; one reference is on Page 14 of the Carpentry Contract. In the February 19, 1894, edition of the *New York Daily Tribune*, an interview with architect Fred Camp discusses in detail the air exchange system "of about 5,000 cubic feet of air per minute by use of fans." The final source is the big wooden pipes themselves - 440 feet in length - that are present under the Auditorium floor.

The Carpentry Contract details the construction of a floor and ceiling ventilating duct system for the removal of air from the Auditorium and "as needed could be operated by fans run by steam." The ventilating system consisted of 10 grates about 4 feet by 5 feet. The gratings were either "oak or yellow pine with holes 2 inch by 2 inch, allowing an aggregate of openings in all the 10 gratings to be 80 square feet." Three circular wooden tubes 5 feet in diameter ran from the floor grates to the front of the Auditorium (west to east), where they were to be secured to the iron frame of a fan. The wooden tubes were made of tarred hemlock planks held together by "galvanized band iron with screw lugs, or by ¼ inch round wire iron, galvanized twisted together and clinched about 3 feet apart." Currently there are six closed grates on the floor with four open grates in the ceiling.

While the specifications list "10 floor grates," the 1894 Annual Report also states that "the floor has 48 iron ventilators to create an air current beneath and also prevent the decay of timbers." Humidity was a consideration: the movement of air through the 48 floor registers provided necessary moisture reduction under the floor and assisted in air flow.

By natural convection, air rises to the ceiling and exits through the four ceiling grates, each measuring 10 foot square: one under the west tower, one over the choir platform, and two at equal intervals in between. The air exited the building via the two large main towers and the two side roof

The black rectangle painted under the seats shows a sealed floor vent of the north pipe. It extended into the aisle, but is now covered with floorboard and carpet.

A view from the attic, looking down through the ventilation grate. It is a 55 foot drop to the floor.

dormers. The "Doctor Breeze" was also effective when the east doors were open. Unfortunately, these door entrances were closed, creating areas under the interior balcony steps which are now a music room on the north side and a preacher's room on the south.

The two smaller towers on the Auditorium front have open louvers at the top and sealed wooden shafts that extend down two stories to two brick-lined chambers (approximately 10 feet by 10 feet) which were connected to the wooden ventilation tubes. It appears that the natural sea/land breeze was of such movement on Ocean Pathway that the air entered the two smaller east towers, moved through the tunnels under the main floor and exited out the floor registers into the Auditorium. Assisted by the three tiers of open doors and windows, this interior draft naturally rises up 55' to the four ceiling registers and exits out the two larger towers and side dormers. The heat from numerous human bodies also contributed to the air movement.

Notes in two places in the margins of the Carpentry Contract - Ventilation Duct (page 14) state "Alterations made before signing." This suggests that the ventilation system was changed, but we don't know exactly how. We do know that the installation of the Hope-Jones Organ (1907-1908) resulted in the tunnel ventilation system being cut and partially removed. One or two old timers recall iron floor grates on the main floor (not wood, as per the contract) with air flowing out of the grates up to the ceiling. These were sealed when the new theatre seats were installed in 1961. Some ushers remember the 48 small cast iron grates around the perimeter of the Auditorium. These grates were also removed and the openings covered.

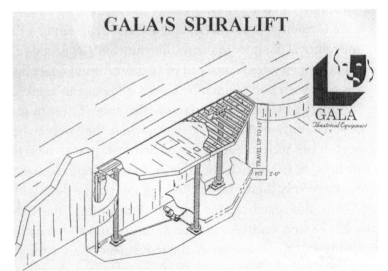

GALA'S SPIRALIFT

The Gala Spiral Lift (2001) is one modernization that interrupted and exposed the big wooden ventilation pipes. The drawing shows the elevation system. Its mechanism is installed under the stage in a trench lined in concrete block. The wooden pipes still remain on each side of the trench.

Crawling Beneath the Auditorium Floor

The 2001 installation of the Gala System Stage Lift made it possible to investigate more fully the Auditorium's ventilation system. Excavation for the stage lift's service pit (under the altar rail and the main platform) exposed the remains of three abandoned air duct tunnels, each about five feet in diameter. The tunnels are partially filled with excavated sand from the Gala System installation, yet youth worker Tim Miller was able to crawl into the south tunnel for 42 feet, where he could see a brick wall about 30 feet further into the tunnel. The five foot tunnel decreased slightly in diameter toward the west end, and there were two overhead grate openings that were sealed. Viewed from the main level, one can observe the outline of these sealed grates, marked by straight cuts in the wooden flooring. One grate on the north side is partially outlined in black paint. The outlines of the covered grates are not obvious in the present aisles because the Andrew-Demarest chair count of 11 per row, replaced by new theater chair count of 12 per row, changed the aisle configuration.

In this photograph of the stage elevator mechanism, the platform and choir loft are to the right and the auditorium floor is to the left (west).

In 2008, Gerry Gironda crawled all the way to the west end of the Auditorium along the outside of the middle tunnel to install cable controls for the new Echo Gallery Organ. He reports a smaller tunnel present at a 45 degree angle from the middle tube. The sketch of the tunnels provides more detail.

The mystery of the Auditorium ventilation system is that we don't quite know how the system worked: changes were made in the specifications, large air ducts were cut, and there is no evidence of fans in the basement (as indicated in the contract). There are two brick chambers in the basement that were connected to the towers and may have housed the fan units. Either the fans were never installed, or they were removed at a later time. An additional mystery is that the Milliken Contract calls for the furnishing of a coal shute; its purpose is not evident. We do know, however, that the oft-told myth of a long tunnel running underground from the beach to the Auditorium for the purpose of bringing fresh air to the assembled worshippers is just that – a tall tale. It is the natural sea/land breezes which makes it so pleasant to live in a seashore community.

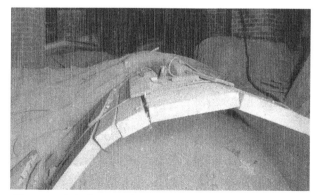

Photograph looking to the east under the stage, taken while standing in the elevator trench. Note the cut end of the south pipe; sand in the pipe is from the stage lift excavation.

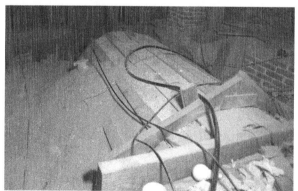

Here is a portion of the north pipe under the stage, looking east.

Still looking east, one can see the south pipe and the south diagonal which connects to the center pipe. The south pipe originally led to the tower, until a large section was removed to accommodate the 1907 Hope-Jones organ.

The brick base of the north tower at one time included a large hole, now bricked in. The hole is the size of the wooden pipe and in line for connecting with the north pipe. The connecting pipe, and possibly a fan, had to be removed to accommodate the 1907-1908 organ installation

Science and Speculation

This completes the description of the observable facts, but let us add some science and careful speculation to complete the story. Begin with a couple of facts from science: (1) Warm air is less dense than cool air and therefore, warm air rises and cool air falls; and (2) air will not move horizontally without some motive force. These facts explain what occurs between the floor and the roof vents: the hot air is vented through the roof. However, as the floor is now sealed, the only source of cool air is the three tiers of open doors. A northerly or southerly breeze greatly improves the effect.

But what was it originally? In speculating on the exact configuration of the Auditorium air flow, we begin at the outlet, because we know more about that. It is clear that the ultimate fate of the heated air was to exit the Auditorium through the two large towers (front and rear) and the two side dormers. Warm air rose to the attic and to these outlets via the four ceiling grates that are visible today.

Auditorium Manager Chris Flynn points to one of the wooden bands that ties the pipe boards together.

Now the intriguing question: how did cool air originally flow into the Auditorium? There are two ideas. First through the many doors around the walls, including the first floor doors which were to be raised up under the second floor balcony. Recalling the big wooden pipes, it would seem clear that cool air flowed through the north and south wooden pipes and vented into the Auditorium through the large floor vents. It is also reasonable to conclude that the air entered these pipes somewhere under the stage.

Additionally, the air at the top of the smaller towers at the front of the Auditorium would be cool, certainly cooler than the interior of the Auditorium, and cool air would tumble down these towers into the pipes described earlier.

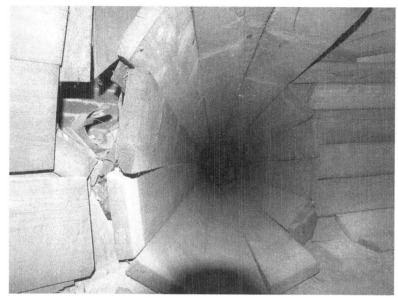

This close-up photo shows the connection between the north diagonal (off to the right) and the north pipe, which continues straight ahead to the bottom of the north tower. However, the two small towers no longer assist in ventilation.

This is the cut made in the south pipe for the stage elevator. Once again, sand from the excavation was placed in the old pipe.

The second idea for cool air flow is a bit more esoteric: recall the 48 small iron grates around the Auditorium's perimeter. It is very likely that the cool air from the surrounding wooded areas drifted into the Auditorium through the open doors and down through these grates into the center wooden pipe. This pipe does not have grates into the Auditorium and splits in two on its way to the rear of the building. While there are two potential sources of cool air under the stage, we do not know how the air traveled to the north and south pipes and then into the Auditorium, although we have some educated guesses.

Mystery: What Fan?

The early photos and drawings show the pipes all connected together, and the science supports the flow of air through the various interconnected pipes and out through the roof vents. Architect Fred Camp mentions a fan in his 1894 interview. Where was it? Was it ever installed or was it eliminated before the building was finished? Were there two fans? We are unable to find any clear evidence. For the fan to function properly, it needs to be placed between the cold air sources and the pipes that carried the air under to the Auditorium floor (the north and south pipes). No likely placement exists as the pipes are presently configured. If the blower were at the junction of the north and south diagonals and the center pipe, it would effectively move air from the 48 iron grates to the floor vents, but would tend to force air back up the two front towers. If there were two fans, one at the base of each tower, they would effectively force air to the floor vents via the north and south pipes, but would also force air up through the 48 iron grates. Neither of these two alternatives would work well. It is doubtful that there were three fans, as balancing the air flow from them would be problematic. It is possible (but unlikely) that the pipes were configured differently than they are today. Perhaps the fan was eliminated before or after building completion because the builders realized the problems described previously. We don't know: we have looked, crawled into pipes, bumped our heads to get a better look, risked our ears while looking under the organ pipes while Dr. Turk practiced, and still we don't know. The authors welcome any additional information that would preclude some or all of the speculation by verification or contradiction.

The south pipe again; note the construction of the pipe, which was all done on site. We don't know the purpose of the wheel-like assembly lying in the sand. The best idea offered is that it is part of the sound effects generator for early 20th century productions of "The Storm."

Ventilation Today

Today a large movement of air is still present in the ceiling at the main east tower. There are times, particularly on a summer morning, when air movement is very rapid from the surrounding wooded parks and tent area into the Auditorium. Church worshipers often complain about being cold when the rear doors are open. Through the design of movable doors and hinged panels, ventilation ducts, grates and soaring towers, Frederick Camp brilliantly resolved the major complaints regarding the previous Auditorium. The roof no longer leaked, the sun did not shine in one's eyes and the ever-present breezes made one feel cool and comfortable in the new shaded seats. A person sitting inside this great hall would find that the surrounding green woods and white tent grounds visible from within the structure reinforced the spirit of the open-air camp meeting assembly. The Auditorium was not a church but a spectacular open-air tabernacle!

Today, looking out at Front Circle from a seat in the Auditorium. Photo by Paul Goldfinger.

Appendix

Acknowledgments:

In today's world, one must rely on supportive help to create and produce a book on the history of anything. This "Great Auditorium" was such an undertaking. We thank all – the Authors.

Kathy Arit; Shirley Bell; Richard Beltle; Keith Bigger; Frederick Branch; Dr. Arthur Chesley; Sam Ciccarella; Richard Deetz; David Dougherty; Harvey Downing; Ginnie Dufresne; Harry Eichhorn; Chris Flynn; Lew Daniels; David Fox; Dr. Paul Goldfinger; Jack Green; Jack Green, Jr.; Phil Herr; Stephen Hirt; Nancy Hoffman; Scott Hoffman; Pam Iodire; Judy Kaslow; Ken Keating; William Kresge; Sam LaRosa; Chris Neuffer; Anna Nichols; George Olson; Derek Parish; Wendi Powell; Christina Powell; Katie Powell; Rev. Walter Quigg; Martha Rakita; Susan Roach; John Rouleau; Harriet Russomano; Raymond Russomano; Robert Ryerson; Gary Saretzky; Jon Schmitz; Rev. Dr. Harold Schmul; Jenny Scott; John Shaw; David Shotwell; Howard Smith; Kelly Story; Mary Jane Schwartz; Kelly Truitt; Dr. Gordon Turk; Zoe Waldron; Bill Zimmerman.

And The Ocean Grove Camp Meeting Association; Historical Society of Ocean Grove; the Monmouth County Archives; Monmouth County Historical Association; Hofstra University; Asbury Park Public Library; Sarasota (FL) County Library; New York Public Library; Brooklyn Public Library; Saratoga (NY) County Library; Chautauqua (NY) Institution Archives.

The authors gratefully acknowledge the contribution of the Ocean Grove Refreshment Staff towards the publication of this book.

The Great Auditorium Refreshment Service

Bonnie Ayres, Penny Bates, Shirley & Ted Bell, Justin Billings, Carol Brooks, Dot Conselyea, Linda Conselyea, Fred Ohleth, Pat & Tom Darnsteadt, Barbara Davies, Edward Drzewiecki, Kim Francione, Mike Gerdes, Beverly Hubbard, Sheree Hutcherson, Ruth Lyons, Jean & Lou Mitchell, Elaine & Derek Parish, L.J. Rogers, Dee Van Housen, Gaye Williams, Pete Wool.

In memoriam: JUDY RYERSON and JAKE VAN HOUSEN

AUDITORIUM TIME LINE

FIRST CAMP MEETING OF TEN TENTS - JULY 31, 1869

Charter issued by State of New Jersey on March 3, 1870, to the "Ocean Grove Camp Meeting Association of the Methodist Episcopal Church." Initial purchase of land, lot lay out and sale of individual 99 year leases of 30 by 60 foot lots, and location of auditorium/church square on 1870 map.

1870	First preaching stand, 24 by 24 feet, seating 75 ministers, surmounted by a small but sweet toned bell. Total cost: $800. Congregational seating – 1,000 people on pine plank, one and a half inch thick, planed on both sides and edges without back. 24,000 feet total. All preaching held in an open grove of pitch pine and oak woods.
1873	Preacher's stand enlarged and improved. Cost $200.
1874	Congregational grounds reseated with park settees. 150 purchased from the New Jersey Conference Camp Meeting Association at Pitman Grove, NJ. Cost $750. Other seats, cost $425. Total $1,175. Small bell removed, replaced by 600 lb. bell made by Jones & Co, Tory, NY. Cost $250. Altar rail installed.
1875	A substantial frame erected, 75 feet by 100 feet, covered with green pine and laurel bowers. Strong opposition to installing covering roof.
1876	Covering roof installed – September.
1880	Auditorium enlarged, 136 feet long by 146 feet broad. Center posts raised from 13 feet to 24 feet high, side wings 18 feet high, seating coverage of one half acre for 3,400 adults, new platform and camp chairs – 800 seats, total 4,200 seats. Cost $7,800. Attendance estimated at 6,000 or more on Sabbath days.
1882	Two story building, 20 feet by 30 feet erected in place of old reception room, back of old stand. Cost $800. Full cellar, with home gas arrangement for auditorium illumination. Building included janitor's office, minister's room and two spacious upper rooms for sleeping.
1883	Stokes begins to urge the reconstruction of a new larger auditorium for an audience of 8,000-10,000 people.
1884	Roof re-covered with Johns Fireproof Coating. 60 new settees, some 20 feet long, seating additional 700 people, accommodations for 5,000 people.
1886	Sounding board installed. Cost $54.43.

1888	August 3: gas chandeliers and five electric lights used in Auditorium.
1891	Model of proposed new auditorium built by General J. C. Patterson & Janitor Wistar H. Stokes, plans by W. H. Carman, Esq., too costly. One lady, unasked, handed to Rev. Stokes $100 in gold towards a new auditorium.
1892	Continued discussions on need for new auditorium.
1893	Finally on May 9, 1893, a resolution by the Trustees was adopted to begin the process of fund raising and design of new auditorium. Resolution conditions include the following: Auditorium to be completed by July 1894. Seating capacity for ten thousand persons. If possible, costs not to exceed $50,000. "That in order to avoid a cumbersome debt we will not commence said building until two-thirds of the amount needed is secured on reliable subscriptions." Sunday, August 13, 1893, was named as "Auditorium Day" for the purpose of raising funds. This special day involved morning, afternoon and evening services which resulted in $41,500 as pledged for the new auditorium. Wistar H. Stokes was appointed by the Association as Secretary of the Building Committee with instruction to keep proper minutes, accounts and a Day Book.
1893	August 14: Issued a call through the public newspapers for plans for a new auditorium, size 150 feet by 230 feet, to accommodate 10,000 people. September 11: Received 15 plans and estimates, including the Berlin Iron Bridge Company, Wrought Iron Bridge Co. of New York, and F.T. Camp. October 10: Fred T. Camp's design accepted; J.T. Wills listed as Camp's associate. October 16: Removal of old auditorium by work crew of 6-8 men. October 28 at 4 P.M. Last of the columns taken down. No injuries to workmen. Janitor's building removed and sold for residence. Received $367.64 from sale of old auditorium lumber. Some timbers were used for construction at the South End pavilion. November 29: Articles of Agreement for Iron-work, Milliken Brothers, NY, NY. Ground broken for foundations on Dec. 2, 1893. The total excavation for the New Auditorium was reported at 173,934 square feet or 6,442 cubic yards as directed by Captain L. Rainear, Superintendent of Ocean Grove. This excavation involved the careful sculpturing of a gentle sloping bowl (225 feet by 161 feet) to a rough depth of 8 feet at the center of the altar rail located at the eastern end of the new building. One row of tents on north side of auditorium removed.

1894	February 1894: Foundations of broken stone mixed with cement, set with a granite cap stone for truss base. George Potts, Esq., donated the granite cap-stones from his own quarries in Pennsylvania.
	March 6, 1894: First of seven trusses installed.
	March 19, 1894: Last of trusses in position. Eighteen angle trusses for balcony installed.
	March 28, 1894: Iron-work completed; average of 30 workmen. Carpenters began their work.
	A ventilation system of registers and 440 feet of wooden tunnels was installed to provide air movement under the floor. A hard pine floor was constructed over the three tunnels on a support system of brick piers and timbers. The center of the Auditorium floor is about 6' below the outside ground level. This slope provides all occupants with a full view of the speaker on the raised platform.
	June 20, 1894: Auditorium completed in 92 days. Carpenters took their tools and went home. Acoustical demonstration given by Rev. Ellwood Stokes.
	July 1, 1894: Opening of Auditorium.
	August 9-12, 1894: Auditorium dedication, second fund raiser of $26,000. Total cost of Auditorium, $69,112.16.
	August 30, 1894, 3:30 P.M.: Laying of Cornerstone, Placed in a copper box was a list of all contributors to the Auditorium as of August 30, 1894, as well as other memorabilia.
1895	Installation of first organ (2,000 pipes in size), donated by the Washington Square Methodist Episcopal Church of New York City.
1897	Rev. Ellwood H. Stokes died on July 17, age 82, at his home at the corner of Pitman and Beach Avenues in Ocean Grove, New Jersey.
1905	Death of Frederick T. Camp on September 19, age 56, at home in Bloomfield, New Jersey.
1907-1908	Installation of Hope-Jones Organ. Major addition to front (east elevation) to enclose porches, add second floor office, meeting, toilet and dressing room areas. Extensive alterations to choir area to accommodate pipes of the new organ.

1909-1974	Installation of electric American flag at center of choir loft (1914-1917). Stage, altar, choir loft area modernized several times (1934, 1961, 1969), closed central stairway access to choir area to accommodate styles of worship, enlarged organ loft and increased number in choir.
1946	Installation of lighted cross on east tower in memory of those who died in World War II.
1961	Installation of theater seats on main floor.
1976	Designation of Ocean Grove as a National and State Historic District*
1979	Removal of *Ocean Grove Auditorium* sign from roof.
1980	Installation of fire alarm and automatic sprinkler system of entire building at a cost of $277,429.16.
1986	Interior electric upgraded to meet current electric code. Old system based on knob and tube wiring. Roof installation of terne coated stainless steel roof, non-reflective warm gray color, replacing corrugated aluminum, snow shields installed. Total cost $687,306, State of New Jersey Historic Grant, $250,000. Original roof was sheet iron.
1993	Interior ceiling cleaned and restored, much of 1961 "modernization" removed to reveal original altar rail and wainscoting of the interior walls.
1994	Installation of iron finials on towers.
1999	Choir seats replaced by a gift of $60,000 from the Ocean Grove Refreshment Staff, a group of 15+ volunteers who sell bottled water, soda (including sarsaparilla), hot dogs and candy on entertainments nights at the Great Auditorium.
2001	16 Cluster lights around balcony reinstalled, gift of $17,000 raised from the Annual Ocean Grove Restoration Ball. Installation of a Gala Spiralift, a forestage lift, for a 253 square foot floor area (46 feet by 5.5 feet) between the altar rail and the platform. This electric lift represents a significant cost saving in labor on the manual assembly and disassembly of the stage extension.
2004	Further restoration of roof decking, gutters and leaders, sidewalks.
2008	Celebration of 100 years of the Hope-Jones Organ. New Echo Gallery Organ installed.
2011	Main tower refurbished by a gift of $40,000 from the Ocean Grove Refreshment Staff

* Town of Ocean Grove, HABS No. NJ1007, NR; and the Auditorium, HABS No. NJ1007-A

The Great Auditorium Name

The term "Great Auditorium" truly defines this building, yet it took a while for this phrase to come into common usage. A review of over 100 years of Ocean Grove publications and newspapers seem to support this statement. It was during the OGCMA presidencies of Phil Herr and Jim Truitt that emphasis was placed on the expression. Credit goes to Jim Lindemuth, a public relations person, who was the business manager at the OGCMA at the time, and to Kelly Truitt who volunteered as the Saturday night entertainment hostess at the Great Auditorium.

1894-1896 FINANCIAL STATEMENTS

Stokes' promise was to have all costs of the new Auditorium paid for by outside donations and not as a budget item of the Camp Meeting. After three years of solicitations the debt was reduced to $1,566.50. After Stokes' death in 1897, the annual appeal for these funds was never again mentioned in the Annual Reports. Included here are the three financial reports from the 1894, 1895 and 1896 Annual Reports.

TWENTY-FIFTH ANNUAL REPORT (1894)

TWENTY-FIFTH ANNUAL REPORT.   59

The financial statement is as follows:

Cost of new auditorium, including, furniture, and
    everything pertaining thereto, all and singu-
    lar, inside and fixings outside, as grading,
    curbing, lights, etc., etc., - - - - $66,610.68

Add, donations, work, material, etc., aggregating*   2,501.48

        Grand total cost, - - - $69,112.16

Whole amount subscriptions in public and pri-
    vate, from first to last up to Nov. 14th, 1894,
    10 A.M., - - - - - - - $73,275.65

Whole amount of subscriptions paid to Nov. 14th,
    1894, at 10 A. M., cash, - - - -   56,243.01

Received from donations of work, material, etc.,   2,501.48

And material from old building sold, - -   367.64

      Total receipts, - - - - $59,112.13

Remaining obligations, Nov. 14th, 1894, 10 A. M. $10,486.05

To meet these obligations, take whole sub. of - $73,275.65

And subtract therefrom cash received, $56,243.01

Amount for persons who say they did
    not subscribe, or are dead, -   -   698.00

Persons who were asked by mail to
    pay subscriptions, letters re-
    turned, unopened - - -   384.50

Duplications on our books amount to   1,617.00

Without addresses, amount to -   -   2,295.50

      Total deductions,   - -   61,238.01

      Balance, - - - - $12,037.64

*Donations as follows:

Miss E. E. Smith, Bible and Hymn Book,	$ 10.00
John Osborn, and wife, curbing and Corner Stone,	61.48
L. D. Wilkinson onyx slab,	50.00
J. S. Flitcroft & Bro., plumbing,	200.00
George Potts, granite for foundation piers,	1,500.00
A. H. DeHaven, electric motto	250.00
A. H. DeHaven, hymn books,	280.00
Mrs. Bishop, Simpson Baptismal font,	150.00
	$2,501.48

TWENTY-SIXTH ANNUAL REPORT (1895)

New Auditorium. You will, I know, all of you, be greatly interested in knowing the exact financial condition of this great building. In July last, knowing as I did, the exact financial situation, I prepared, and caused to be set forth in large readable letters, neatly framed, and hung conspicuously to public view, on the east front of the building, the following, which explains itself:

$3,000 SHORT

This Auditorium cost (with everything pertaining thereto), $70,000. Of these $70,000, $67,000 have been collected and paid; hence, as stated above, $3,000 short; no less; no more. To meet these $3,000, we have in unpaid subscriptions, made in August, 1893, and at the Dedication, August 9 to 12, 1894, about $4,000; these last subscriptions mainly in small sums, we find almost, if not quite, impossible to collect for the following reasons: Some of the subscribers have departed this life and are with God; others are in adverse circumstances, acknowledging the validity of the claim, but to their regret, unable to pay. More than one-half of the above amounts, however, is with persons whose residence we do not know, and consequently cannot communicate with them. It is possible that the *reader* may be one of this latter class; if so, it would be a great relief to us if they would report to W. H. Stokes, Secretary of the Building Committee, at the Janitor's office, or the undersigned. It may be too, that someone advised of these facts, and not having had an opportunity previously to contribute to this great work, would be willing to help us in this emergency. Any amount will be thankfully received by the Secretary, and applied to meet the deficiency now overdue.

E. H. Stokes, *President*

Ocean Grove, N. J., July 20, 1895

This notice, which has been read by thousands, it will be seen, bears date, July 20, 1895. Since its issuance, up to the present, (Nov. 13, 1895), there have been received, $1,091.63 on the $3,000 note now due to which is to be added six months' interest. It should be noticed, however, that not much more than fifty per cent, of the amount has come from delinquent subscribers. The other part from new contributors. Many thanks to all. The balance, $2,000, with added interest, until paid, is unprovided for, only as from time to time we may succeed in picking up a few dollars from these old subscribers.

TWENTY- SEVENTH ANNUAL REPORT (1896)

New Auditorium. – We have now occupied this great structure for three summers. It grows favorable upon most people each time it is revisited. It is possible that if we had the work to do now, with no more light that then, we would do no better, if as well. Its capacity is not too great, often not up to our needs. With the vast majority of visitors, whatever may have been their previous impressions or prejudices, on seeing, criticism is disarmed and objections lost in praise.

I regret to say there yet remains a debt upon it of just $2,000. This I had fondly hoped would have been liquidated last summer; but times were dull, and other financial matters pressed. Please note as follows:

NEW AUDITORIUM REPORT, NOVEMBER 11, 1896

Amount of cash of hand November 11, 1895,	$1,091.63
Amount cash paid, $1,000 on $3,000 note.	
" interest " $90 " " due: November 15, 1895.	1,090.00
" cash balance on hand November 15, 1895	$4.63
" cash received from old subscribers to May 15, 1895.	105.00
Total	$106.63
Paid interest on $2,000 note, due May 15, 1896	60.00
Balance cash on hand May 15, 1896	$46.63
Received cash from old subscribers since May to November	
11,1896.	71.50
Total	$118.13
To pay interest, 6 months on $2,000 note, due November 15, 1896.	60.00
Amount cash on hand November 15, 1896.	$ 58.13

Amount of unpaid old and new subscriptions.	$2,433.00	
Amount less receipts.	166.50	
	$2,266.50	
Of which amount there promises to pay.	700.00	
Amount very doubtful.	$1,566.50	

W. H. Stokes, Secretary, New Auditorium Fund

Tree Planting and Landscaping Around the Auditorium

The OGCMA Annual Reports have numerous references to the role of trees and a yearly "Tree Planting Day." Stokes always emphasized that Ocean Grove reflected two words, "Ocean" and "Grove." The sea is always there, but the grove of trees that covered the camp meeting grounds was gradually removed to accommodate new roads and cottage construction. To Stokes the absence of trees diminished the name of Ocean Grove. A grove in Stokes' view was also a sacred place or "Holy Ground," where meaningful events in one's life had happened. One of his annual ventures was a tree planting ceremony.

Here is a report from April 25, 1894, of a simple tree planting ceremony of 11 trees around the Auditorium:

Young saplings line Front Circle in this early photo. Note the open door on the north-east face – once an entrance for both people and breezes, now closed in for the music library.

A line of trees was planted between the Auditorium and the first circle of tents on Mt. Pisgah.

Tree Planting Day: An Anniversary Peculiar To Ocean Grove

The Association Plants Trees to the Honor and the Memory of Departed Fellow Laborers in the Master's Vineyard – Hon. James Black, Miss Martha Weston, Joshua Peacock and Others Remembered. From *Wednesday's Daily*:

This is tree planting day in Ocean Grove.

To the accompanying music of the hammer and the saw, and with the shapely outlines of the great auditorium as a background, beautiful, straight and arrow-like trees were planted to the memory of Ocean Grove's honored dead.

The trees were places at stated intervals all around the immense building. Dr. E.H. Stokes conducted the services, which were attended by a number of ladies, the pastors of the Grove churches and several members of the Association. Dr. Alday made the opening prayer.

First to be honored was Hon. James Black of Lancaster, Pa., one of the original members of the Ocean Grove Association. Mr. Black died at his Pennsylvania home last winter. President Stokes said of him that he was a man who never allowed heat or cold, tempest or calm, to keep him from a duty. "With a soul larger than his body, although his body was the largest among us," said President Stokes, "he never counted a duty too laborious to perform."

The Association members joined hands on the first shovelful of dirt and cast it in to the memory of the dead associate. The ladies gathered up little handfuls of dirt and threw them in the excavation. A hymn prepared especially for the planting ceremonies was sung at each excavation.

The second tree of honor was named for Miss Martha Weston, whose pocketbook was always open. She died in New York two weeks ago. Joshua Peacock, whom none knew but to love and none named but to praise, and who died only yesterday, was awarded third place. The fourth tree was named for Mrs. Elisza Cooper, a daughter of sorrow and affliction who came to Ocean Grove at an early period in its history. Chaplain Gilmore, who lived in God's favor and died in his favor, was fifth on the roll of honor. Miss Martha Jones came next.

And so it went from tree to tree. The namesakes of Rev. James Matthews, Wm. H. James, ex-Sheriff Allen and Thomas and Letitia Price are even now making their rapid and mysterious growth in the shadow of the great Auditorium. A kind word of eulogy, a tender remembrance from friends of loved ones was said at each excavation.

And so it continued from tree to tree until a total of 11 trees were planted.

Landscaping and Urns

In 1894, one way of landscaping a town like Ocean Grove was with huge cast iron urns. Urns were often given as permanent memorials for loved ones, and were occasionally relocated due to expansion of streets or sidewalks. For example, there were originally two urns in front of the Auditorium as shown in the 1894 dedication photo (Chapter One).

Today there is only one urn on the north side, by Front Circle. Here are examples of urns in Ocean Grove, maintained with flowers for the summer season by the Beautification Committee of the Ladies Auxiliary of the Auditorium Ushers.

The "Memorial Vase," built by the Fisk Ironworks Company, is located on the corner of Surf and Central Avenue in Founder's Park (once called Memorial Park). This marks the location of the Thornley tent where the first Camp Meeting service was held in July 1869.

1869.   MEMORIAL VASE,   1875.
UNVEILED AT
OCEAN GROVE, NEW JERSEY,

The "Pioneer Ladies" Urn (above left) with three dolphins attached at the base was originally in front of the Auditorium. It is now located at the intersection of Broadway and Central Avenue.

This urn, (above right) on the northeast corner of the Auditorium, was originally located on the southeast corner.

ADDITIONAL AUTHOR NOTES

All illustrations are by Darrell A. Dufresne, unless otherwise noted. Copies of pictures and illustrations can be obtained by contacting the authors at the Historical Society of Ocean Grove, c/o PO Box 446, Ocean Grove, NJ 07756 (phone 732-774-1869 or FAX 732-774-1685) or email to: info@oceangrovehistory.org. Website: www.oceangrovehistory.org.

Missing Historical Items

Where is Wistar Stokes' Day Book?

Wistar Stokes, whose cousin is Ellwood Stokes, was appointed keeper of the Day Book, in which every event concerning the building of the new Auditorium was recorded. This included requisition and dispersion of building materials, payment to contractors and workers, and daily progress of construction. This book was known to be in the Camp Meeting Office as late as the 1980s. Loaned out to interested parties, it was never returned. Knowing how meticulous the Camp Meeting was in keeping records, this book is invaluable to recording the history of the building of the Auditorium. Do you have the Day Book??

No issues of the Ocean Grove Record, Spring 1894?

Rev. Wallace Adams, as editor of the *Ocean Grove Record*, was a true lover and supporter of Ocean Grove's mission. His weekly newspaper provides us with careful and thoughtful details of life in Ocean Grove, as he reported activities both in and out of the Auditorium. His issue of Saturday, August 5, 1893, featuring a front page drawing of a proposed building, was strategically timed to be in local hands just before the fund raising day. But the *Record* strangely ceased publishing with Vol. XX, No. 4, on January 27, 1894, and reappeared on April 14 with this note on the editorial page: It is a real pleasure to see the clean cut *Ocean Grove Record* once more, and to know its valued editor is again in his sanctum. We can only surmise that Rev. Wallace was ill; despite his boundless energy, he was unable to publish during February and March of 1894, and we miss his astute input about the construction of the Great Auditorium.

Further Reading

Alpern, Andrew (1996). *Historic Manhattan Apartment Houses*, Dover Publications Inc., Mineola, NY

Aron, Cindy S. (1999). *Working at Play: A History of Vacations in the United States*. New York, NY: Oxford University Press.

Auditorium Theatre of Roosevelt University, (2010) Congress Parkway, Chicago, Ill.

Bell, Cindy L. (2008). *Ocean Grove Auditorium Choir: A Faith-Based Community Chorus*, 2008 ISME CMA Seminar, Rome, Italy.

Bell, Wayne T. (2000). *Images of America, Ocean Grove, NJ*. Charleston, SC: Arcadia Press Publishing.

Bell, Wayne T. & Flynn, Christopher M. (2004). *Ocean Grove in Vintage Postcards*. Charleston, SC: Arcadia Press Publishing.

Bell, Wayne T. & Goodrich, Margaret (1975). *Nomination of Ocean Grove as a State & National Historic District, 1975-6*, Neptune Township, New Jersey.

Bender, Roger & Stowell, R.R. (2008) *Chimneys: A Natural Ventilation Alternative for Two-Story Barns* AEX-115-98, Ohio State University, Columbus, Ohio.

Brewer, Richard E. (1976). *Perspectives on Ocean Grove*, R. Brewer, Ocean Grove, NJ.

Bristol, Frank M. (1908). *The Life of Chaplain McCabe: Bishop of the Methodist Episcopal Church*. New York: Fleming H. Revell Co.

Brown, Kenneth O. (2001). *Dr. Elwood H. Stokes – The Father of Ocean Grove*. Hazleton, PA: Holiness Archives.

Brown, Kenneth O. (1997). *Holy Ground Too – The Camp Meeting Family Tree*. Hazleton, PA: Holiness Archives.

Camp, F. T. (1882). *Draftsman's Manual on How Can I Learn Architecture?* NY: W. Comstock.

Carter, Kate B. (1967). *The Great Mormon Tabernacle*. UT: Utah Printing Company.

Cody, Jeffrey W. (2003). *Exporting American Architecture - 1870-2000*. New York: Rutledge Press, NY.

Crocker, Kathleen & Currie, Jane (2001). *Chautauqua Institution - 1874-1974*. Charleston, SC: Arcadia Publishing.

Daniels, Morris (1919). *The Story of Ocean Grove – 1869-1919*. New York: The Methodist Book Concern.

Finke, Roger &. R. Stark (1992). *The Churching of America - 1776-1990*. New Brunswick, NJ: Rutgers University Press.

Fogelson, Robert M. (1989). *American Armories - Architecture, Society, and Public Order*. Cambridge, MA: Harvard University Press.

Fox, David H. (n.d.) *The Journal of William B. Milligan – 1894-1917*. Ocean Grove, NJ: Historical Society of Ocean Grove.

Fox, David H. (1992). *Robert Hope-Jones*. Richmond, VA: The Organ Historical Society.

Fox, David H. (2003). *The Ornaments of Ocean Grove*. Ocean Grove, NJ: Historical Society of Ocean Grove.

Gibbons, Mr. & Mrs. Richard F. (1939). *History of Ocean Grove, 1869-1939*. Ocean Grove, NJ: Ocean Grove Times.

Gorham, Barlow Weed (1854). *Camp Meeting Manual: A Practical Book for the Camp Ground in Two Parts*. Boston: H. V. Degen.

Hughes, George (1873). *Days of Power in the Forest Temple*, Boston, MA: John Bent & Co.

Hughes, Glenn (1951). *A History of the American Theatre – 1700-1950*. New York: Samuel French.

Irwin, Alfreda, L. (1987). *The Chautauqua Story*. Chautauqua, NY: Chautauqua Institution.

Kenton, Amanda Gail, (2004). *Natural Ventilation in Auditorium Design; Strategies for Passive Environmental Control.* Proceedings of the 21st Conference on Passive & Low Energy Architecture, Eindhoven, the Netherlands.

Kaufmann, Edgar, Jr., ed. (1970). *The Rise of American Architecture.* New York, NY: Metropolitan Museum of Art, Praeger Publishers.

Kirkegaard Associates, Report-*Audio Systems Design - Great Auditorium, Ocean Grove, NJ* (2003) KA Project #1924, Chicago, Illinois.

Kramer, George W. (1897). *The What, How and Why of Church Building.* New York: Geo. W. Kramer, FAIA.

Kresge, William, Editor and Publisher, *Ocean Grove Record/Times, 1874-1989*, Ocean Grove, NJ.

Landau, Sarah Bradford & Condit, C.W. (1996). *Rise of the New York Skyscraper, 1865-1913.* New Haven, MA: Yale University Press.

Meeks, Carroll L. V. (1956). *The Railroad Station - An Architectural History.* Mineola, NY: Dover Publications, Inc.; reprint of Yale University Press.

Messenger, Troy (1999). *Holy Leisure – Recreation and Religion in God's Square Mile.* Minneapolis, MN: University of Minnesota Press.

Milliken Project # 3366, *Drawings and Specifications of Steel Work - #571, Auditorium*, Ocean Grove, NJ, 1893.

Milliken Brothers (1905). 1905 Catalog. NY: New York.

Minutes of the Newark Conference of the Methodist Episcopal Church, Newark, NJ. 1894.

Minutes of the Newark Conference of the Methodist Episcopal Church, Newark, NJ. 1895.

Morrill, George P. (1971). *The Multimillionaire Straphanger, a Life of John Emory Andrus.* Middleton, CT: Wesleyan University Press.

Morrison, William (1999). *Broadway Theatres – History and Architecture.* Mineola, NY: Dover Publications, Inc.

National Park Service (1991). *An Historic Theme Study of the NJ Heritage Trail Route* –Chapter III, Religious Resorts.

Ocean Grove Camp Meeting Association Annual Reports, 1870-2011, Ocean Grove, NJ.

Osborn, W. B. (Mrs.) (1915). *Pioneer Days of Ocean Grove.* New York, NY: Methodist Book Concern.

Rose, Delbert R, (2000). *Vital Holiness.* Nicholasville, KY: Schmul Publishing Co.

Sackett, John (1917). *Scannell's New Jersey's First Citizens and State Guide.*

Schlereth, Thomas J. (1992).*Victorian America - 1876-1915.* New York: Harpers Collins Publishers.

Sterngass, Jon (2001). *First Resorts - Pursuing Pleasure at Sarasota Springs, Newport and Coney Island.* Baltimore, MD: John Hopkins University Press.

Stokes, Ellwood Haines (1898). *Footprints In My Own Life.* Asbury Park, NJ: Pennypacker Press.

Vanderweil, Gary (1976). *Draft Heating and Ventilating Systems of the Victorian Era.* Victorian Society in America, Spring 1976, p. 14-18.

Newspapers

Asbury Park Press, Daily Journal, Daily Press, Shore Press, Ocean Grove Record, Ocean Grove Times,1880 - 1980

New York Times (1857 – Current File); ProQuest Historical Newspaper; The New York Times (1851-2003)

Brooklyn Eagle, Brooklyn, NY, 1893-1894

New York Tribune, New York, NY, 1894

About the Authors

Wayne T. Bell, Jr., resident of Ocean Grove, NJ, since 1970, is semi-retired from a nearly five decade career in environmental research, historical report preparation, grantsmanship and education. A noted speaker in New Jersey, he is recognized for his lectures and demonstrations on such subjects as American Pattern Glass of 1830 to 1910, Stained Glass Windows, Victorian Architecture, Wildflowers of New Jersey, and the History of Camp Meetings. Recent publications include *Images of Ocean Grove* (Arcadia Publishers, 2000), *Ocean Grove in Vintage Postcards* (Arcadia Publishers, 2004), and the popular pamphlet *So How Old is My House?* (Historical Society of Ocean Grove, NJ, 2003). Mr. Bell was the lead author in the 1976 proposal that designated the Ocean Grove Camp Meeting as a National Historic Site, and was a contributing author to *Encyclopedia of New Jersey* (Rutgers University Press, 2004).

Each summer, Mr. Bell volunteers his time and knowledge to the Historical Society of Ocean Grove, leading interpretative tours on the Auditorium grounds or assisting as a Curator and Historian. He also served as a member of the Historic Preservation Committee for the Township of Neptune, which reviews and approves applications for restoration of Victorian structures within the Historic District of Ocean Grove. During the winter months, he volunteers as a docent at the Sarasota (FL) Historical Society in Pioneer Park.

Cindy L. Bell is Associate Professor of Music Education and Director of the 140-voice University Choir at Hofstra University in Hempstead, NY, where she also teaches undergraduate and graduate courses in music education, general music, and choral music methods.

As a specialist in choral music education, teacher training and community choirs, she has published articles in numerous music journals and presents professional workshops for Long Island and New York City schools, as well as for state, regional and national music organizations, including NYSSMA, MENC, ACDA and ISME. A fifth-generation Ocean Grover, she enjoys returning each summer to guest conduct in the Annual Adult Choir Festival, the largest sacred choral festival on the East Coast, featuring a choir of 800 voices. Besides working with her father, Ted Bell, writing the history of the Great Auditorium, she is researching the musical programs of Ocean Grove and the Camp Meeting tradition, and presented a paper on the Auditorium Choir for the International Society of Music Education's Community Music Seminar in Rome in 2008.

Darrell A. Dufresne is recognized for his keen interest and research in history and archaeology, with emphasis on the science and engineering applicable to historical times and places. An engineer by profession, with an advanced degree in business, Mr. Dufresne is an avid student of history, and enjoys applying his dual interests in history and engineering to each other.

Mr. Dufresne has visited ancient Roman archaeological sites in Italy and England, in addition to research via historical collections and publications. As resident of Ocean Grove, NJ, and a member of the Historical Society of Ocean Grove, he takes full advantage of the society's collection of Victorian era artifacts and records. The Great Auditorium is a specific interest to him and provides the unique opportunity for much amateur archeology and application of science and engineering.

CPSIA information can be obtained at www.ICGtesting.com
Printed in the USA
LVOW022159261212

313368LV00002B/82/P

9 781614 930365